BRITISH
COACHING

Chassis Manufacturers, Coachbuilders and Operators

To John.

Happy Birthday

from

Fiona.

xx.

BRITISH COACHING

Chassis Manufacturers, Coachbuilders and Operators

MICHAEL HYMANS

AMBERLEY

First published 2016

Amberley Publishing
The Hill, Stroud
Gloucestershire, GL5 4EP

www.amberley-books.com

British Library Cataloguing in Publication Data.
A catalogue record for this book is available from the British Library.

ISBN 978 1 4456 6180 3 (print)
ISBN 978 1 4456 6181 0 (ebook)

Typeset in 10pt on 13pt Sabon.
Typesetting and Origination by Amberley Publishing.
Printed in the UK.

Contents

Introduction

It was while browsing through my collection of old bus and coach photographs that I realised how many famous makes and models of coaches have disappeared from our streets. Perhaps the most iconic was the Bedford OB, with the driver sitting behind the protruding bonnet with a gleaming chromium-plated radiator grille. But other famous names are also distant memories: Duple, AEC, Bristol and even Leyland.

I remember in my home town of Eastbourne, the seafront would be lined with coaches touting for business. This would be in the heyday of coaching – the late fifties and early sixties – before many families could afford their own car, and long before foreign holidays became available to most.

Blackboards would be leant against the sides of the coaches, showing their destinations and cost. 'Afternoon tours to top of Beachy Head for 5s' – or 'Evening mystery drive with stop at country pub for 7s 6d'. Competition was fierce with local firms, like the Jackson Bros, who kept their blue coaches immaculate, vying for passengers with larger companies like Southdown.

Sadly these are now scenes of the past.

There is still a living to be made for smaller coaching companies, however. Bookings are more often than not done online or by phone and perhaps a larger percentage of work is for social clubs and private charters. Many coach firms supplement their income by ferrying children to and from schools, a result of many village schools closing their doors.

So what became of these businesses and, indeed, how did they start? This book sets out to give a history of the best-known brands. It is not exhaustive; apologies if your favourite tour operator is not mentioned.

In using the images, I hope I have not breached any copyright – apologies if I have. If my apologies are not enough, please contact the publisher and any necessary corrections will be made at the first opportunity.

Chapter 1

Stagecoaches

The comfortable air-conditioned coaches capable of running at 70 mph are a world away from travel 300 years ago. Roads were single-track, muddy affairs that caused problems should two carts meet head on, as passing places were a rarity.

In 1703, when Charles, King of Spain, visited Petworth House in Sussex, it was reported that his coach capsized and had to be supported on both sides by peasants. Improvements were very slow and, in Elizabethan times, roads were still reported as having many hazardous rocks and valleys.

When improvements to these tracks were suggested, there was a certain amount of local opposition, including petitions to parliament, as it was forecast that better roads would bring 'cut-throats, footpads and undesirable characters' to the area.

In Sussex, where I live, one of the first stagecoaches served Lewes, the county town. This was in 1756. It was a stop on the London–Brighton (then called Brighthelmstone) route. It was advertised as 'The New Flying Machine' and could carry four passengers, making the entire journey in just one day and starting from Charing Cross at six o'clock in the morning. Fares were not cheap, costing 13s to Lewes and 16s to Brighton. Budget airlines were not the first to limit the amount of luggage allowed, as only 14 lbs per passenger was allowed on this stage.

Sussex roads had a very bad reputation (some things never change) and in the 1760s circuit judges refused to attend courts in Lewes during the winter months, as roads were generally impassable.

In 1816, a trip was advertised as only taking six hours between London and Brighton, 'under penalty to passengers'. This meant that the horses had to be galloped all the way. Inevitably, this led to many accidents and Sir William Cosway was thrown from a stage and killed. In one week, more than a dozen horses were driven to their deaths. Measures were soon taken to put an end to these trips.

By 1880 there were four journeys each way on this route, including one overnight trip. Just over ten years later, there were thirty trips each way on the route.

A stage waits to leave the Burlington Hotel in Eastbourne with a full load of passengers.

At the heyday of the stage, over 150,000 horses were needed to pull the stages on routes that criss-crossed the country.

One of the longest trips by a stagecoach was between London and Edinburgh. The journey took two days and used about 100 horses, which were changed twenty-seven times at coach houses on the route. These coach houses employed many staff, including ostlers, to take care of the horses (the term was a variant of hostler – one who worked at a hostelry) and cooks to take care of the passenger's needs. The fastest ostlers could turn a stage round in two minutes. The stages kept to strict timetables and many stops were only long enough to enable the horses to be changed, but others had catering facilities to feed the travellers, and some even had overnight facilities where passengers could get a decent night's sleep before continuing their arduous journey the following day. Some of the busier coach houses catered for up to twenty stagecoaches calling every day.

Mail coaches were the fastest stages of the day, with many having four, rather than two, horses. They were the most lucrative for the coach houses and many vied for the contracts and did their best to give a good, efficient service. The last mail coach ran in the 1850s, when it was replaced by the railways.

The stagecoaches that ran where there was no competition from the railways lasted until the start of the twentieth century, when the advent of the internal combustion engine led to their demise.

Another stage at a South Coast resort – this time Brighton – and the London stage is about to depart via Redhill.

Chapter 2

Charabancs

The word 'charabanc' derives from the French *char-a-banc* and dates back to horse-drawn vehicles in the nineteenth century. Its definition was a long wagon with forward-facing benches.

There does not appear to be any record of when the first motorised charabanc was built, but it was early in the twentieth century when the internal combustion engine took over from horse power. The ride was probably no better than in horse-drawn days, with solid tyres still being used. Many companies and drivers did not like operating during the hours of darkness, as street lighting in many areas was poor or non-existent, and the lighting on the vehicles left much to be desired. Headlamps were either still lit by acetylene or, for more modern machines, electric lighting worked by commutators driven by the engine. This meant that the faster the engine went, the brighter the lights became, but driving slowly meant very dim lights. Some side/tail lights were still lit by oil and these had a nasty habit of going out.

Batteries were still not standard on charabancs and so starting the engine meant that it had to be cranked over by hand, using the starting handle at the front.

Antifreeze had yet to be invented, so radiators had to be drained overnight. Refilling them with hot water made the oil a bit thinner, meaning it was easier to crank the engine.

During the Second World War, the manufacturers of charabanc chassis had all their output taken by the War Department. Dennis supplied 7,000 chassis, Leyland 6,000 and Albion Automotive of Scotland 5,000, which were fitted with lorry bodies.

After hostilities ended, there was a massive surplus of these chassis and many ex-servicemen saw the opportunity to purchase one or more, fit them with charabanc bodies and start up in business for themselves. Many used them as dual-purpose vehicles and also built lorry bodies that could be exchanged with the charabanc bodies that were used primarily during summer months, reverting to lorries in the winter. Some even swapped them on a weekly basis; lorries on weekdays, charabancs at weekends.

Waiting outside the company's offices in Eastbourne was this solid-tyre charabanc with acetylene lighting. Judging by the clothing of the passengers, they were expecting a rather cold, uncomfortable journey.

Two charabancs full of soldiers stand outside All Saints Hospital in Eastbourne, which was used for recovery and recuperation of those wounded in the First World War.

Although many firms stayed as small family businesses, some expanded and acquired a fleet of charabancs. One such company was Chapman's of Eastbourne. They were the first company to run tours. By 1911 they were running tours to Cornwall and Scotland and, by the 1920s, with a fleet of thirty-six charabancs, continental tours were being undertaken, travelling as far as Italy. The fleet increased to fifty vehicles throughout the decade, with the majority being supplied by Dennis.

Improvements to vehicles were made, the most notable of which were pneumatic tyres and electric lighting. Protection for the passengers improved as well, with side windows being introduced and roofs that could be rolled backwards for sunny days and kept up for inclement weather. The later charabancs resembled the early motor coach.

Journey times were much longer in those days and comfort stops had to be taken on the way. Some hostelries did very well from this, for example The Felbridge at East Grinstead on the way to Eastbourne, and the Black Swan at Pease Pottage on the Brighton run. Any other comfort breaks had to taken on the roadside – ladies to the left and gentlemen to the right!

This is one of the later charabancs. It had the luxury of pneumatic tyres, electric headlights and windows. The roof was retractable, but could be pulled up during inclement weather. This shot was taken on the road to the top of Beachy Head from Eastbourne's promenade.

As time marched on, some companies became larger, eventually becoming household names. Operators had a choice of chassis available, with a range of engines, petrol or oil, that could be fitted. Bodies could be supplied by a host of coachbuilders. This led to a wide and interesting range of coaches being seen on the country's road. The following pages detail the rise and eventual fall of a once-thriving industry.

Chapter 3

The Chassis Builders

AEC

AEC, or the Associated Equipment Company, was formed in 1912 in London by the Underground Group, which itself had taken over the London General Omnibus Company. It was set up as a separate entity to concentrate on the manufacture of buses. They were based in Walthamstow, at premises first set up by the Motor Bus Construction Company in 1905. By the time they were taken over by AEC, they were building thirty Type B chassis every week.

The X type had also been in production since 1909, but the outbreak of the First World War saw manufacture concentrate on building lorries for the war effort. The same chassis was utilised for both buses and lorries.

In 1926 there was an amalgamation with Daimler, but this was short lived due to problems with Daimler's engines and differences in management styles. The association was ended in 1927, although the two co-operated with each other in future years.

Although AEC supplied all of London's buses, they had few other orders; the Walthamstow premises were too large for just this output and smaller premises were sought elsewhere. A new site was found at Southall in West London and the newly built factory was fully functioning by June 1927. This site was large enough to enable expansion and new workshops and departments were opened regularly up to the outbreak of the Second World War.

Production included a range of lorries as well as buses. Their buses had names starting with the letter 'R' including Regent, Regal and Renown. A new badge was designed. This incorporated the red-and-white AEC logo into a blue triangle. In the 1950s a winged design was incorporated into the badge.

Early chassis were all powered by six-cylinder petrol engines but, in the 1930s, an eight-cylinder engine was trialled. Five engines were built but were unsuccessful; they were removed from the buses that trialled them, which then reverted to the six-cylinder design.

An AEC Regal III, sporting coachwork by James Whitson & Co. Ltd and owned by Duval's of Kingston, a company taken over by Epsom Coaches in the 1980s.

This AEC Reliance was fitted with the last body to be made by Windover. It was delivered to Gillet Bros of Quarrington Hill, Durham, in 1955.

A 1952 Burlingham-bodied AEC Regal IV, owned by Blue Ensign of Doncaster.

The offside view of another Burlingham AEC Regal IV, this one owned by Don Everall of Wolverhampton.

In May 1929 a Regent was run around Brooklands motor-racing circuit for twelve hours. It covered 507 miles, averaging 43 mph and returning fuel consumption of 7.5 mpg. The Regent was officially launched at the Olympia Motor Show in November, along with a Regal chassis and four lorry chassis – the Mercury, Majestic, Monarch and Mammoth.

The first batch of 250 Regents were bought by companies nationwide, including: Birmingham Corporation who bought twenty-eight bodies by Brush; Nottingham, who had twenty with English Electric coachwork; Halifax, who had six bodied by Shorts; and London General Omnibus Company, who had two. These became ST1 and ST2. Regents were also to be seen on the streets of Chester, Oxford, Glasgow, Watford and Truro.

Alongside the Regent, the single-deck Regal chassis was being produced, which was suitable for dual-purpose use.

1932 saw the introduction of a revolutionary new chassis – the Q chassis. This had the engine mounted on the offside, just behind the front axle. The floor extended about 4 feet forward of the front axle, allowing passengers to board right at the front. Although many of these were used for local bus services, many found their way to operators of long-distance routes and coach operators. Indeed, the first examples off the production line were bodied by Duples and purchased by Elliott Bros of Bournemouth. Other Q chassis received coachwork by Harringtons, Willowbrook and Weymanns. The design did not prove to be successful and production finished in 1937. Only thirty-seven doubles and 319 singles were produced. One of the reasons for their short life was that, with the engine mounted behind the driver, it protruded into the passenger compartment. This meant that the front seats on the offside had to be mounted longitudinally. This may have been acceptable on short bus journeys but not on longer coach trips. Duple overcame the problem by creating high floor designs with the seating above the engine, but the changes were not enough to make the chassis design viable.

RT1 was built in 1938 with an 8.8-litre engine coupled to a German Bosch pre-select gearbox. This chassis carried an old open staircase body, previously used on Leyland Titan TD111. It entered service as ST1140.

During the Second World War, production was again switched from producing buses to concentrating on building lorries to transport goods and troops.

A new body was being designed and built at Chiswick works, which was fitted to RT1 in 1939. 338 were ordered, but the outbreak of war had limited these to 150, with the last one not being delivered until 1942. Production recommenced in 1946, with 4,674 being delivered between 1947 and 1954.

2,131 other RTs were produced on Leyland chassis. 1,651 were classified as RTLs, which had longer chassis, and 500 were RTW, which had 8-inch wide chassis, rather than the standard 7.6 inch. The last RT to survive in

A Willowbrook-bodied AEC Reliance, built in 1961 and operated by Potteries Motor Traction.

Greenslades of Exeter operated this AEC Reliance with Duple body.

service was RT624, which operated on service 62 out of Barking Garage on 7 April 1979.

In 1948 AEC acquired Crossley Motors and the Maudslay Motor Company, and so Associated Commercial Vehicles Ltd was set up as a holding company. Their vehicles were still badged as AECs.

In 1953 AEC introduced a new vehicle, with its engine mounted under the floor. This was the latest version of the Reliance – a name first introduced in 1928 on a front-engine bus that was the first one to carry the famous blue triangular badge. The Reliance was a medium-weight chassis that became a heavyweight when restrictions were lifted to allow 36-foot vehicles.

The most iconic and successful vehicle built by the company was the Routemaster. This was designed in the early 1950s and went into production in 1956. The vast majority were used in London, but a small number were supplied to BEA and to the Northern General Transport Company. A total of 2,876 were built, and over 1,250 still survive.

Of course, not all production was used in London and the famous AEC blue-and-red logo could be seen all over the country.

In 1962 the company was taken over by Leyland Motors Ltd. Vehicles continued to be built badged as AEC until British Leyland closed in 1979.

Gurney Nutting bodied this forty-one-seat AEC Regal IV, new in March 1953.

This AEC Reliance was owned by Silcox of Pembrokeshire. It had been new to Morrisons of Tenby in May 1955, where it sported green-and-white livery. It was sold to Silcox in December 1958 and repainted in red and cream. It had a Plaxton C39C body. It was sold for spares in October 1970.

Yelloway of Rochdale owned this 1979 AEC Reliance with Plaxton Supreme IV coachwork.

Another of the last of the AEC Reliances to be produced, this time sporting Duple Dominant coachwork. Note the twin doors that allowed a grant to be claimed for vehicles intended for stage-carriage work.

Bedford

Bedford Vehicles was established in 1930 and was the brand name used by Vauxhall for their commercial vehicles. They produced a range of vehicles from light vans to large lorries, as well as coach chassis. Vauxhalls had been part of General Motors since 1925.

The Bedford OB was one of the country's best-loved and numerous coaches. The first examples were made in 1939, but the war soon interupted production with only seventy-three examples being made before the factory had to be switched to the war effort, building Churchill tanks. As soon as hostilities finished, production of the OB resumed and continued until 1951, by which time 12,766 had been produced. They were powered by six-cylinder 3.5-litre petrol engines linked to four-speed manual gearboxes. They could achieve speeds of over 40 mph, which was very good for the time.

Bedford joined forces with Duple to design the bodywork. The bodies, named the Vista, were made using a combination of ash wood and reinforced steel, with the floor being tongued and grooved boards. Seating capacity was normally twenty-nine, with luggage being stored in the boot or overhead racks. The cost of a new coach was just over £1,300, depending on specification.

Royal Red coaches' Llandudno Bedford OB coach.

A superb array of enamel signs form the backdrop to another Bedford OB, this time owned by Warner's Luxury Coaches.

A 1966 Bedford J2 with Duple Compact coachwork. It was owned by the Royal Household and used for staff transport.

This is a 1958 Bedford SB3 coach, fitted with a Yeates Europa body and owned by Alpha Coaches of Brighton.

Barton's of Nottingham owned this 1963 Bedford Val 14, fitted with Yeates DP56D bodywork.

In 1950, Bedford exhibited the replacement to the OB at the Commercial Motor Show. It was called the SB and differed from the OB in that it was a forward-control design, with the driver sitting alongside the engine rather than behind it. This meant the end for traditional half-cab designs, and full fronts, which looked far more modern, became more and more common.

Purchasers of SBs were given a choice of engines. Bedford's own petrol engine was still available, but a Perkins or Leyland diesel could also be fitted. Bodywork was not restricted to Duples either and a choice of Plaxton, Harringtons, Willowbrook or Marshalls was available.

The Bedford VAL was introduced in the mid-1960s and was immediately recognisable as it had twin front axles. Over 900 examples were built between 1963 and 1966. In 1967 the coach came with a larger 7.64-litre engine. This was designated the VAL70, superceding the VAL14 that had the smaller engine. Many were fitted with Duple or Plaxton bodies, but smaller coachbuilders like Harringtons or Yeates also used them.

The demise of Bedford was due partly to losing the contract with the army to supply 4-ton trucks. This contract was awarded to Leyland DAF. With increasing competition from abroad in both trucks and coaches, the decision was taken to cease production of Bedfords and the factory in Dunstable closed in 1986.

Royal Red Coaches of Llandudno owned this 1965 Bedford VAL coach, registration BCC 795C.

Bristol

This section on Bristol's coaches could have been put in the chassis, body-builders or operators section of this book, because they performed all three tasks.

In 1875 the Bristol Tramway Company operated its first horse-drawn trams. In 1895 it introduced its first electric trams. In 1906 it started operating motor buses as feeder routes to its tram services. Two years later it built its first bus chassis for its own services and soon expanded into building chassis for other operators. Their first customer was Imperial Tramways of Middlesbrough, who ordered a charabanc. The reason for gaining this order was that the two companies shared the same chairman, Sir George White, and when a rival company in Middlesbrough started a competitive service, he used some of Bristol's buses to combat this threat.

The company not only built buses but other commercial vehicles, and one early order came from the Royal Navy Air Service.

Expansion meant that new larger premises were needed and these opened in Kensington Hill Brisington. It was known as the Motor Constructional Works.

In 1929 the tramway company was bought by the GWR and the bus services were sold to Western National in 1931. This brought the business under the control of the Tilling Group. Many of the chassis were used by Eastern Coach Works of Lowestoft, another member of the Tilling Group, and chassis had to be driven across the country with no protection for the poor drivers.

BHU 92C, original fleet number 2138, was a Bristol MW69 with an ECW dual-purpose body. It entered service in 1965, serving until July 1970 before being sold. It has now been preserved.

British Commercial Vehicles were created in 1943 as a subsidiary to Bristol Tramways. 1948 saw nationalisation of the bus industry, with the passing of the Transport Act and the formation of the British Transport Commission. This restricted sales of BCV to other BTC operators.

1956 saw the end of production of bodies by Bristol Commercial Vehicles. That year the Leyland Motor Corporation was allowed to buy a stake in Bristol and this opened up a wider market to them, but the last Bristol-badged chassis to be built was a double-deck VRT/SL bus. This was in 1981. Chassis continued to be built at the factory, albeit with Leyland badges, until October 1983 when the last vehicle, a Leyland Olympian, left the factory, bound for ECW to be fitted with a body for Devon General.

Commer

Commer started life in 1905 as the Commercial Car Company in Lavender Hill, South London. It was always a manufacturer of commercial vehicles, with its first offering being a van.

The founders wanted to go into production of larger vehicles, so new premises were found at Biscot Road, Luton. Their first lorry was produced there in 1907 and their first bus followed two years later.

As with most vehicle manufacturers, the First World War put an end to all civilian production and the factory turned its attention to making military vehicles for the British Army. Post-war, the company's finances were never too good, with the firm going into receivership on many occasions before, in 1926, it was taken over by Humber, which in turn became part of the Rootes Group in 1931.

Commer originally produced their own engines before using the Rootes TS3 diesel engine, which became known as the Commer Knocker due to the distinctive sound the three-cylinder engine made. Later vehicles could be purchased with a choice of Perkins or Cummins engines.

After the end of the Second World War, the company produced the Avenger and Commando models. Rootes were taken over by Chrysler Europe in the 1970s and their vehicles were badged as Dodge's. In 1978 Chryslers were purchased by Peugeot and vehicles were produced in partnership with the commercial division of Renault.

A 1951 Commer Avenger II chassis, with Churchill C34C bodywork, run by Royal Red coaches of Llandudno.

This Commer Avenger II coach was fitted with a Churchill body, similar to the previous image but with slight detail differences.

Dennis

Dennis can trace its history back to 1894, when John Dennis moved from his home in Devon to Guildford to work for a firm of ironmongers. He also started building bicycles from proprietary parts – the Speed King for gentlemen and the Speed Queen for ladies. This proved so successful that he gave up his job in the ironmongers and opened his own business called The Universal Athletics Stores, trading from a shop in the High Street. The business became enough of a success that his brother, Raymond, soon joined him and they opened a workshop behind the retail premises.

They foresaw the future in motorised transport and, in 1898, they strengthened one of their tricycle frames and fitted a French-made De Dion engine to it. Trying the new contraption out in the high street, John fell foul of the law as he was accused of driving furiously at 16 mph on his new machine. How the police measured his speed is not related, but his exploits cost him a fine of 20s. He turned this to his advantage, as he used this case to prove to prospective purchasers his machine's performance.

The two brothers formed a private company, Dennis Brothers Ltd, and continued building motorised vehicles. They added another wheel to their tricycles to produce a quadricycle, which was the forerunner to their first motor car.

Expansion meant moving to even bigger premises, and new offices and a factory were acquired at Onslow Street in Guildford. They exhibited their first

Chapman's of Eastbourne started their business running horse-drawn bus services in Eastbourne, but moved into motorised transport when the opportunity arose. Not only did they run local services, they also ran a daily service to London.

motor car at the Motor Show held at Crystal Palace in 1904. That year they not only produced their first van, which they supplied to Harrods, but also made their first passenger-carrying vehicle. This was powered by an Aster 28 hp engine and ran on service between Kingston-upon-Thames and Richmond.

Supplying this wide range of vehicles meant moving to even bigger premises. These were at Woodbridge Hill on the outskirts of the town and this was their final move, with the site meeting their requirements for about ninety years.

Many vehicles of the time were chain driven and the Dennis brothers were not a fan of this method and joined with Thomas Tilling to design a worm-driven axle. This proved to be much quieter and more reliable than chain-driven vehicles.

A range of passenger vehicles were produced, which shared their chassis with a range of commercial vehicles. A 28 hp charabanc cost £535, while a 35 hp double-decker would cost £800.

The company had changed engine suppliers to White & Poppe of Coventry – a company that they subsequently bought.

Just prior to the First World War, the company realised that there was less competition from manufacturers of commercial vehicles than private cars and the decision was taken to cease manufacture of the latter, with the last car being produced in 1913.

During the Second World War, the company experimented with electric propulsion, using internal combustion engines to power electric traction motors.

Chapmans of Eastbourne had a fleet of Dennis charabancs in the 1920s, this is a publicity shot set up in Devonshire Place, Eastbourne. The company was a pioneer of package holidays and ran trips to Cornwall and Scotland, before venturing further afield with trips to the continent. During the First World War, they also converted some of their charabancs to run on coal gas, which was carried in a large bag on top of their vehicles.

The company joined forces with Tilling Stevens to develop this invention and the vehicles manufactured were marketed as Dennis-Stevens. Cardiff Corporation was one of the first operators to buy these, taking delivery of six single and six double-deckers. They were not successful, however, and both manufacturer and operator reverted to more conventional buses.

The war years had been good to Dennis, with the factory working to capacity in order to supply vehicles for the war effort, but the end of hostilities brought much harder times. Not only did orders for new vehicles dry up, but there was also a glut of army vehicles appearing on the second-hand market. Many soldiers adjusting to life in civvy street were buying these to start up in business for themselves. Not only were they being used for the transport of goods, but alternate charabanc bodies were built that could be fitted to the chassis at weekends to run excursions.

The 1920s saw new designs being produced. Until then, lorries and buses had used the same chassis, but a new bus chassis was developed and this had a lower ride height. Pneumatic tyres replaced solid ones, giving a much smoother ride. Greyhound of Bristol introduced a new long-distance bus service to London, using Dennis's new 4-ton chassis. In London it was the police who regulated the capital's buses and they did not allow double-deckers to use pneumatic tyres until 1928, as they were unsure of the consequences of a bus getting a puncture.

A forward-control bus – where the driver sits beside the engine rather than behind it – was introduced. This created more room for the passengers. By the end of the decade many municipal operators were using Dennis buses and they were a common sight throughout the country.

The 1930s saw major changes during a time of recession. The engine factory at Coventry was shut with production moving to Guilford. New homes had to be built for those staff wishing to transfer south. Oil-powered or diesel engines were being developed for use in larger commercial vehicles.

A double-deck Lance and single-deck Lancet were introduced. These sold well throughout the 1930s. For those needing a smaller vehicle, the Dennis Ace was introduced in 1933. This was a twenty-seater that shared its chassis with a small lorry. Coach operators were not forgotten and the Arrow Minor was introduced in 1935. This was not a success though and only forty-five were sold. A new Falcon chassis was introduced in 1938 with a choice of length to carry twenty or thirty-two passengers.

1939 saw the deaths of both John and Raymond Dennis, as well as the outbreak of the Second World War. The government, through the Ministry of Supply, instructed vehicle manufacturers what they could build during the war; all bus production was put in the hands of Daimler and Guy, while Dennis had to concentrate on lorries, with orders coming from the War Office. This brought an end to the production of Lances, Lancets and Falcons.

After the end of hostilities, bus production restarted. The population was enjoying the freedoms of peacetime and, with car ownership not available to the

A 1929 Dennis Falcon, operated by Southdown.

masses, they relied on public transport. Many small coach operators favoured the Lancet. Dennis fitted their own bodies to some, but it was commonplace for operators to buy a chassis and have another company design and fit their own bodies. Many of these were powered by Dennis's own new six-cylinder diesel engine, the O.6, although the choice of other engine manufacturers, like Gardner, was an option.

Buses were to go through radical design changes, with front-engine vehicles falling from grace in favour of vehicles with engines mounted under the floor. This configuration meant that buses could have increased carrying capacity. The Dominant was Dennis's first design, which used a horizontally mounted O.6 engine. In 1952 the Lancet UF was introduced as a lighter version of the Dominant. Four years later, the Pelican was introduced, which was even lighter, but by then Dennis had been losing its market share to Leyland and AEC. Bedford's were also producing lightweight coaches.

The next few years saw Dennis combining with Bristol to build a low-roofed double-decker. Bristol had been nationalised and could not sell to private companies, so Dennis built their Lodekkas under licence and marketed these as Lolines. By the 1960s, bus operators were favouring front-entrance, rear-engine vehicles and Dennis were not producing any. Falling sales of lorries meant that, in 1965, the company was no longer profitable and the decision was taken to halt all bus production and concentrate all their resources on lorries.

In 1972 Hestair Ltd took over Dennis, changing its name to Dennis Motors Ltd. Five years later the name was changed again to Hestair Dennis Ltd.

The new management began to return the company to profitability and was looking to widen the range of vehicles offered. Leyland was the market leader of buses, having bought out AEC, but this rationalisation had decreased the choice available to customers, many of whom were unhappy with the range of vehicles available. A decision was taken to re-enter the bus market with a new rear-engine vehicle. One of the major expenses for operators of bus fleets is the amount of brake wear encountered with stopping every few hundred yards. To overcome this, a Voith automatic gearbox fitted with a retarder was used. This was coupled to a reliable, economical Gardner diesel engine. Leyland rear-engine buses were suffering from overheating problems, so Dennis placed their radiator at the front. This new design was tested by fitting the new drive train to an old Daimler bus. While this was being road tested by a number of operators, engineers at Guilford were designing a brand-new chassis. The first one was ready in 1977 and this received a double-deck body designed by East Lancashire Coachbuilders. The bus became a favourite with many operators, from Scottish Bus in the north to Eastbourne Buses on the south coast. It was called the Dominator.

A Dorchester model was then introduced. This was aimed at the middle-to-long distance market and used a manual, rather than automatic, gearbox. A lighter version was then introduced and the Lancet was once again a name that could be seen on the front of a Dennis bus. The Falcon was a name that was also re-introduced, appearing in 1980 on a chassis that could be used for single or double-deck bodies.

The 1980s saw deregulation of the bus industry and Dennis realised that there would be many new cost-conscious companies looking for new vehicles. Many coaches of the time were using under-floor mounted engines, but these were taking up valuable luggage space, so they developed a bus where the engine sat as far back as possible, increasing the amount of storage space beneath the seating area. Cummins had also designed a new in-line six-cylinder turbo-charged engine, which was incorporated into the chassis design, and the Javelin was born. The design proved to be very popular with coach operators, both large and small, and by 1994, 1,300 had been sold. Cummins engines proved to be successful and they were offered as an alternative to the Gardner engines fitted to earlier bus models.

In January 1989 Hestair sold out its vehicle manufacturing side of its company to Trinity Holdings. Despite the recession of the 1990s, the company built new premises capable of increasing production to the north of Guildford.

The late 1980s saw many operators turning to minibuses to operate their services. These were not popular with the travelling public as they had been derived from vans and were awkward to board and alight from, especially if carrying shopping bags or pushchairs. Dennis management did not follow the latest trend but derived a midibus that was passenger friendly, but not as expensive as the Javelin. This was the Dart. It found favour with London Transport as a

Eastbourne Buses owned this Plaxton-bodied dual-purpose Javelin. It was not liked by bus passengers due to the entrance steps, nor did it have the luxury of a coach. It found work for a while on an ill-fated service between Eastbourne and Brighton. The service could not compete with the good train service and was consistently badly delayed by long-term road works on the A27.

replacement for the Routemaster, as well as other operators countrywide, where a one-man operated bus was needed to run on frequent timetables.

The 1990s saw another revelation in bus transport – the low-floor vehicle. Dennis used a Lance chassis with independent front suspension to produce a bus with a low floor that extended halfway down the vehicle.

Whereas many of its competitors have ceased to exist, Dennis is still going strong over 100 years since the brothers started their business, and the future looks bright with the Guilford factory producing a wide range of modern vehicles.

Ford

Ford's contribution to coaching was relatively limited for such a large company, with their first coach not being produced until about fifty years ago. This chassis evolved from the Thames Trader in the 1960s. It shared many of its components, including the engine, with the D Series lorry. They were front-engine vehicles being mounted ahead of the front axle. This allowed passengers to board at the front as well. They were built in 10 m and 11 m lengths, being the R192 and R226 respectively. Improvements led to reclassification to R1014 and R1114 and, subsequently, R1015 and R1115 by the mid-1980s.

A 1963 Ford Thames 507E, with Harrington Crusader bodywork.

This is a 1960 Ford Thames, sporting a Yeates Europa body. She was owned by I&E of Kearsley.

Hastings Old Town forms the backdrop to this 1973 Duple Dominant-bodied Ford, belonging to Horseshoe Coaches of Tottenham.

This 1967 Ford, belonging to Alpha Coaches, was fitted with a Duple Viceroy body.

Another Ford Thames with Duple bodywork, but this time a Duple Marauder body.

The coaches fitted with these engines were originally competing against Bedfords and Leylands and then foreign imports from Volvo and DAF.

When the government's subsidies to bus companies were cut in 1979, sales dropped off and, with operators favouring rear-engine vehicles, orders dried up and the last one was built in 1986.

Leyland

Leyland can trace its history back to 1892 when James Summer inherited his father's blacksmiths business in Leyland, Lancashire. James was not content with being just a blacksmith and he designed and built a steam-powered lawnmower, winning a silver medal at the Royal Lancashire Show. He formed a company, J. Sumner Ltd, in 1895. The company then built a three-wheeled car using a lawnmower engine.

Henry Spurrier, who had been working on steam engines in the United States for eight years, joined the company.

They formed a new company, the Lancashire Steam Motor Company, to build new steam vehicles and, in 1899, they produced their first steam bus. It is believed that this vehicle was supplied to the Dundee Motor Bus Company in 1900.

The original workforce of around twenty had grown to 150 by 1902, and the sales of buses had increased so much that larger premises in Hough Lane were found.

In 1905 the company exhibited their first petrol-driven-engine bus at the Commercial Motor Show. They had not been able to produce their own engines by that time, so the bus was fitted with a Crossley motor.

A new Leyland Comet leaves the Burlingham factory.

A 1939 Leyland G6 HVW 217, belonging to the City Coach Company, with Duple FC39C coachwork.

A Leyland PS2, belonging to Corona Coaches. It had originally started life with Grey Green Coaches.

A Leyland PS1, registration number EAY 180, belonging to Browns Coaches in Leicester.

A Leyland Royal Tiger with Duple Roadmaster coachwork, belonging to South Notts Coaches.

By 1907 though, they were fitting their own engines into their chassis, which were known as 'X Types'. The same year the company changed its name to Leyland Motors Ltd.

The Second World War kept the company busy, supplying buses to ferry troops as well as lorries to move supplies. In 1915 all 6,000 lorries produced were for the RAF. After the war, the company was not slow in returning to supplying civilian needs. In 1919 two new petrol-engine buses were introduced – the M1 being a twenty-eight-seater and the O1 being a thirty-three-seater. The ensuing years saw more models being introduced, with lorries and buses sharing the same chassis.

In 1926 the first buses with pneumatic tyres were introduced. They were single-deckers called the Leveret, Lion, Lioness and Leopard, which ranged from twenty-seaters to thirty-eight-seaters. The following year, double-deckers were introduced, branded as Titan. A single-deck version, known as the Tiger, was available.

1933 saw the introduction of the diesel engine, which was available as an alternative engine across the range of buses. The 1930s also saw the gradual change to metal rather than timber for the construction of bodywork frames. Dual-purpose vehicles were also being made, as operators wanted to use their vehicles for excursions at weekends and service work during the week.

For a number of years, Leyland had been trying to sell their buses to the London Transport Board, who had used AEC as its major supplier. Consequently, in 1935, they introduced a new lightweight chassis known as the Cheetah, which was used on the Titan TD4 and Tiger TS7. 100 Titans were sold to the London passenger Transport Board. Eighty-seven Tigers, classified as TFs and renowned for their quiet and smooth operation, also entered service in the capital in 1939. For the second time in twenty-five years, production of civilian vehicles was halted due to a world war. This was a shame for many reasons, one of which being that a rear-engined bus called the Cub was being developed, with bodywork being built by London Transport. It had been designated the CR and only forty-eight from the original order of fifty-nine were made before production had to be switched to military purposes. The design never went into production again after the war, and it was twenty years later before the idea of a rear-engined bus saw the light of day again.

After the war, production of vehicles was concentrated on double, rather than single, deckers as there was a dire need to transport as many people as possible. The Titan PD1 and Tiger TS1 were introduced in 1946. The shortage of new vehicles meant that many pre-war buses were refurbished. Petrol engines were replaced with Leyland 7.4-litre oil engines, while old bodies could be replaced with new ones, making virtually new vehicles.

In 1948 the Comet was introduced as a lighter chassis than the Tigers and became popular with small independent coach operators.

1982 Leyland Leopard with ECW bodywork, operated by Eastern National.

Another Eastern National coach was this 1985 Leyland Tiger with Plaxton Paramount bodywork. The design looks far more modern than the first image, and it is somewhat surprising that only three years separate the two vehicles.

This Leyland Tiger Cub operated by Whittle's of Kidderminster was fitted with a Burlingham Seagull body.

There is no indication who owned this Leyland Tiger Cub, fitted with a Duple Brittannia coachwork.

1949 saw a return to the pre-war idea of underfloor engines that gave more room to seat passengers. They worked with Metro-Cammell-Weymann to produce the Olympic and solely produced the Royal Tiger. The Royal Tigers were an instant success and they were built in large numbers.

A lighter version of the Royal Tiger, known as the Tiger Cub, made its debut at the Commercial Motor Show in 1952. It was 2 tons lighter than its predecessor and was favoured by many coach operators. Production of the Royal Tiger ended in 1955.

Newer bus designs were placing the engines at the rear, with the Lowloader and Atlantean being prime examples, but most coach operators preferred the underfloor option.

In 1954 Leyland stopped building their own bodies. Wilkinsons of Sedgefield took delivery of the last Leyland coach body to be built. The Leopard was introduced in 1959 and was a medium-weight chassis designed as a successor to the Royal Tiger. It stayed in production for over twenty years, with many upgrades, such as pneumocyclic and six-speed synchromesh gearboxes, being introduced throughout its life. They were popular with many larger operators, including the National Bus Company and Barton Transport. The government gave grants to operators who bought new vehicles that were built to specific regulations, including width of doors, and stipulated that they had to be used on stage-carriage work for a certain proportion of their working hours. Many Leopards were built with a wider two-piece folding door to meet this specification, which became known as 'express' or 'grant' doors.

Successive relaxations to Construction and Use Regulations over the years had led to longer and wider buses being allowed on the roads. 1961 saw another relaxation of the rules to allow vehicles up to 36-feet long and 8-foot-2.5-inches wide to be built. Constructors were not slow to take advantage of the rule and larger Leopards were introduced later in that year.

1962 saw Leylands take over Crossley, Maudslay, Park Royal and Thorneycroft, and in 1965 they took over Eastern Coach Works.

Although a new chassis called the Panther was introduced, coach operators mainly stayed loyal throughout the 1960s to the Leopard.

1968 saw the formation of the British Leyland Motor Corporation, which was an amalgamation of the Leyland Motor Corporation and British Motor Holdings, and the following year they joined with the National Bus Company to build a new single-deck bus. The result was the Leyland National, which made its debut at the 1970 Commercial Motor Show.

The Atlantean was introduced in 1972 but the relative success of these vehicles could not stop the financial decline of the company and, by 1974, government help was needed in order for it to continue trading. In 1975 Leyland Bus & Trucks became a separate part of the company, although any profits made were used to subsidise the failing car side of the business, leaving a shortage of investment to introduce newer buses.

It was not until 1977 that a new chassis – the Titan – was introduced and a further three years before a successor to the Atlantean – the Olympian – was introduced at the Commercial Motor Show.

1981 saw another split in the Leylands make-up, with Leyland Bus being made a separate entity, although still answerable to its parent company. That year a new version of the Tiger was introduced. It differed from the original, being a mid-engined rather than front-engine model. The depression of the 1980s saw a slump in sales of buses with the only bus being produced, the Olympian, selling only 177 in 1987.

National Express favoured the Tiger throughout the 1980s, but more and more operators were turning to continental suppliers for their new vehicles. The Volvo B10M chassis overtook the Leyland Tiger in number of sales. Leyland's ability to provide breakdown cover on the continent was seen to be in doubt, leading more British companies offering continental tours to opt for DAF, MAN or Volvos. With these vehicles proving reliable, it made sense for operators to standardise fleets and buy them for their local operations.

The 1985 Transport Act saw the deregulation of bus services and the break-up of the National Bus Company. The uncertainty of the future was part of the reason for a slump in orders for new buses.

Early in 1987 Leyland Bus was sold to a consortium of management and banks. This management lasted just over a year before they sold out to Volvo. Production continued with the Volvo B10M being built alongside the Tiger until 1991 under the name VL Bus and Coach (UK) Ltd, but then the factory at Leyland closed,

This 1984 Plaxton-bodied Leyland Tiger was owned by Coopers Tours of Sheffield. It boasted a toilet and television, which was quite unusual for 1984. (Photo Courtesy Michael Clarke)

ending bus and coach production and marking the passing of the once-famous brand into history.

Maudslay

Maudslay was one of the smaller coachbuilders; it was founded in 1902 by Cyril Maudslay and was based in Coventry. Its original output was internal combustion engines for marine use. These were not successful, so the company switched production to automobile engines, producing both three- and six-cylinder engines. In 1904 the six-cylinder version was 9.6 litres and was used in one of the country's most expensive cars.

They also produced a petrol engine that was used in a railway locomotive operated by the London, Brighton & South Coast Railway.

Their first foray into bus production was in 1905, when they produced a double-decker.

The outbreak of the First World War saw an end to the production of private cars, with the majority of output being lorries for the war effort. After the war ended, production of cars did not resume and efforts remained concentrated on chassis for larger vehicles.

In 1924 they produced a new coach design that incorporated a low-floor chassis. 1934 saw another new design, the SF40, which had the front axle

This 1948 Duple-bodied Maudslay originally had a Whitsun half-cab fitted. It was operated by the Yorkshire firm Ward Brothers of Lepton.

set further back than the engine. This was relatively successful, but again the outbreak of another war halted production.

During the war, some production was moved away to Great Alne, near Alcester, to escape the bombing, which proved to be a shrewd move, as the old factory was bombed with some loss of life. Soon after the war – in 1948, to be precise – the company merged with AEC and Crossley to form Associated Commercial Vehicles Ltd. The name was still used on new vehicles until 1950, but it was then phased out.

Chapter 4
The Coachbuilders

Beadle

Unlike many body builders, Beadles cannot trace their history to pre-motorised transport times. Indeed, the company did not build its first coach body until after the end of the Second World War. Prior to the conflict, however, they had taken out several patents to build buses and coaches using an integral design rather than a separate body and chassis. As with many other projects and plans throughout the country, the war put their plans on hold. After peace

An East Kent vehicle with Beadle body – this one a semi-chassisless Leyland GFN 256.

came in 1945, they set about putting their plans into action. They did not build new vehicles, however, but took pre-war half-cabs and turned them into modern-looking full fronts, using all-alloy integral components pioneered in the making of aircraft fuselages.

Six prototypes were made, which were very well received by the industry. Further savings in weight were then achieved by using smaller, lighter engines and gearboxes, which improved the fuel efficiency of the vehicles. These next four vehicles used a variety of engines, including a Bedford petrol, a Commer petrol and two used Gardner 4LK oil examples.

By 1950, another sixty-two coaches had been built, with fifty using Bedford engines and twelve using Morris/Saurer units. They were purchased by operators throughout the country. Southdown and East Kent were major customers, having often supplied their own chassis to be converted. Various chassis were used, including Leylands, Bedfords, Commers and Dennis. They were sold with names like Canterbury for coaches and Thanet for buses. Production ceased in 1957.

An AEC Reliance, also belonging to East Kent, sports a Beadle body.

A 1957 Leyland Tiger Cub with Beadle bodywork touts for business opposite the pier in Eastbourne. The destination screen is somewhat at odds with the job in hand!

Nestling in the South Downs lies Alfriston. Renowned for smuggling gangs, it was not designed for buses and coaches, as this driver of a re-bodied late-1940s Leyland PS1 was discovering. The vehicle was originally delivered with a Duple half-cab body, before receiving this Beadle full-front modification.

Burlingham

Burlingham's were a coachwork business that took its name from its founder – Herbert Victor Burlingham. He moved to Blackpool in 1928 and leased premises in Bloomfield Road and Bond Street.

The first vehicle he produced was a van for a local butcher, but a coach body soon followed and these became the mainstay of his business. His first vehicles were fitted with canvas roofs and windows that could be wound down to give passengers the full benefit of glorious sunny days, but could become fully enclosed when the weather turned inclement. The comfort of passengers was a concern to him and he even offered a toilet compartment in his specifications.

His reputation of producing quality vehicles grew quickly, not only locally but throughout the country, and he was soon supplying vehicles to operators in Scotland and London. He outgrew his original premises very quickly and, in 1929, opened new facilities in Bank Road, Marton. However, these only sufficed for two years before he had to move to even larger premises at Preston New Road on the outskirts of Blackpool, as well as obtaining premises in Newhouse Road, which were used as repair facilities and a base for production of parts.

In 1930, however, Herbert sold his business to a couple of local businessmen, Richard Eaves and Harry Lowcock. They formed a limited company,

A 1953 Leyland Tiger, registration number RAF 509, with Burlingham Seagull body. It was owned by Hawkeys of Newquay.

H. V. Burlingham Ltd. Herbert moved to Garstang and started producing caravans.

Changes to coach design soon followed with canvas roofs giving way to metal ones – although they could also slide open. Windows were no longer fully retractable, but curved windows were set into the roof above the side windows to increase visibility and light.

Expansion continued and, in 1931, more new premises were needed. A new factory was opened in Vicarage Road. This was used for the final assembly of bodies. Bus bodies were also built, with Blackpool Corporation one of its first customers, buying both single- and double-deck buses.

The 1930s saw a change in chassis design with the front axle set further back. This allowed full fronts to be designed, giving a far more modern look than the traditional half-cabs.

The Second World War brought an end to virtually all coach production. The factory switched production to building frames for Wellington bombers and mobile canteens for use by the armed forces. Towards the end of hostilities, some bus bodies were produced for Barton Transport and Unites Automobile Services.

After the war had finished, there was no shortage of works, as many operators were crying out for new vehicles, although most of the output was for buses rather than luxury coaches. Ribble was one of their major customers. They also ventured into the trolleybus market, building fifteen bodies on British United Traction chassis for Portsmouth Corporation.

The 1948 Commercial Motor Show previewed a new Burlingham designed body, mounted on to an AEC Regal III chassis that was to be used on Scottish Motor Traction's Edinburgh–London service. Other bodies were fitted to Leyland Tiger, Leyland Comet and Commer Commando chassis.

At the 1950 Commercial Motor Show, Burlingham produced two new designs on Leyland Royal Tiger and AEC Regal IV chassis. The AEC coach bore the livery of Woods of Blackpool, who traded as Seagull coaches and had a seagull motif on the sides. This style of body became known as the Seagull coach, with operators ordering Seagull bodies for their new vehicles. It remained popular throughout the 1950s, with large operators including Wallace Arnold and Ribble ordering large numbers of the marque.

Design updates were introduced throughout the 1950s, but these alterations generally had an adverse effect to the good looks of the original. In 1959 a Seagull 60 was introduced for front-engine coaches and a Seagull 70 for underfloor-engine vehicles.

The following year Duple bought out Burlingham's for £550,000, renaming the company Duple (Northern) Ltd. In 1969 Duple closed their Hendon factory and concentrated their entire output from Burlingham's Blackpool premises, but any new designs that emanated from the factory, for example the Continental and Firefly, were badged as Duple. Production lasted there until 1989 when Duple itself was liquidated.

Hawkeys also owned this Burlingham Seagull-bodied AEC Reliance, new in 1955.

Dimbleby's of Ashover owned this Burlingham-bodied Bedford SBG 681 DNU.

Seen in 1960, this was a 1955 Burlingham-bodied Leyland PSUC1 2, registration number FDB 572.

This Burlingham Seagull body was on a Leyland Tiger chassis and was operated by the Pembrokeshire-based firm of Silcox Coaches.

This is one of thirty double-deckers supplied by Burlingham to Ribbles on Leyland PD1/3 chassis in 1948, in order to operate express bus services to Blackpool. They were known as 'White Ladies'.

Their appearance changed in 1951/52, when a different radiator grille was fitted. They were sold in 1959. (Photo Courtesy Michael Clarke)

Another new C33F coach leaves the factory on trade plates. This one was on an AEC chassis, bound for Florence coaches. (Photo Courtesy Michael Clarke)

Duple

Duple can trace its history back to 1919. Herbert White, who had been an ironmonger and farmer, turned his hand to coachbuilding. His original idea was to equip vehicles with dual-purpose bodies, hence the name Duple. This was shortly after the First World War, when there were a lot of commercial chassis available that were originally used on military vehicles. His first effort was to alter an ex-military Model T Ford to be a small touring car, which could have the rear bodywork removed and replaced by a van top. He called his vehicle the 'Bifort'. It was popular with small businessmen, who could have a delivery vehicle during the week and take their families out at the weekend. This principle was later used on larger vehicles by many charabanc builders, who designed vehicles that could be used as lorries during the week, but could have the bodies swapped at weekends to become charabancs. Herbert's first premises were at Hornsey in London before, in 1925, he moved to a larger site in Hendon, Middlesex. The first bodies made there were for charabancs, and then buses, before the company started to produce bodies for luxury coaches in the 1930s. Business was good and, within ten years, they had 800 employees. The company was supplying vehicles to the Great Western Railway as well as Royal Blue.

Wessex Coaches of Bristol owned this 1938 Opel with Duple body.

A 1948 Leyland Tiger with Duple A type C35F bodywork, belonging to Maypole Coaches of Lathom, Lancashire. It had been delivered new to Sutherland Transport at Peterhead.

A 1950s view of a classic Bedford OB with Duple bodywork, belonging to Hants & Sussex.

In the 1930s many smaller operators were put out of business by the introduction of the 1930 Road Traffic Act, which regulated the industry and demanded higher standards. The depression of the 1930s also led to the demise of some of their competitors. Duple stuck to their principles of producing quality vehicles and this proved to be a successful strategy.

The company was helped by an order for fifty bodies from Green Line Coaches, part of London General Omnibus Company, to be fitted to AEC chassis.

The 1930s also saw the continuation of their original business – building bodies for cars – and they fulfilled an order from Vauxhall to body some sports tourers. These were displayed at the 1933 Motor Show in London, as well as smaller orders for Alvis and Buick.

The directors of the company enjoyed travelling around the world, mixing business with pleasure, and were successful in winning orders from the USA, Africa and many European countries.

At home, a large contract was received from the GPO to body their vans. The coaching side of the business continued to expand and larger premises had to be sought. This problem was solved by purchasing 3.5 acres of land adjacent to their existing factory.

1931 saw the start of the long-term partnership with Bedfords, when they received an order to body some of their new fourteen- and twenty-seat chassis. In 1932, Duples acquired London Lorries, another firm of coachbuilders.

A Duple Super Vega on a Bedford chassis, owned by Campings of Brighton.

An unusual vehicle was this 1968 Bedford J2, fitted with a Duple Compact body. They could seat nineteen passengers but were only made in small numbers. Plaxton's also made a body to fit the J2 and this proved to be more popular.

The latter part of the decade saw major improvements in design to coach bodies, with sculptured panels, sloping window pillars and rounded roofs, which gave them a far sleeker appearance compared to the boxier vehicles produced in earlier years.

1936 saw the introduction of a design called 'Vista', which included a sliding roof as well as the above features. This was updated the following year and was called the Vista II. Another design – the Hendonian – was also introduced.

Just prior to the Second World War, Bedford introduced one of the most recognisable chassis – the OB – and Duple lengthened their Hendonian body to fit the longer chassis. Production did not last long, as the outbreak of war meant that most of vehicle manufacturers' production was turned over to the war effort. One of the items produced for the war effort was fuselages for the Halifax bomber. When the war was over, however, coach production restarted and Duple-bodied Bedfords started to become a common sight throughout the country.

1946 saw a change in the company's name to Duple Motor Bodies Ltd.

An 'A Type' body was also produced. This was a half-cab design and in the years following the war, these new bodies were fitted to many types of older chassis as new chassis were in short supply.

Bodies designed for dual-purpose use were also being produced. These were classified as 'B' and 'C' types. Duple had also designed their own bus body that was classified as 'D' type.

Vaggs of Oswestry owned this Duple Midland-bodied Bedford SB.

Austin Hire owned this 1964 Thames Marauder with Duple Commander bodywork.

Royal Red of Llandudno owned this Commer Avenger, with Super Vega body.

Post-war designs started to use entirely metal frames for their bodies. The reason was twofold. Timber was scarce and metal frames were expected to be more durable. The first metal-framed body was called the Almet. Double-deck bus bodies were also built, benefitting from the new technology.

When the regulations were relaxed in the 1950s, allowing vehicles 30-feet long and 8-feet wide to be built, a new range of bodies were designed to suit these. The Roadmaster was designed for coaches with engines mounted under the floor. This was designed exclusively to fit the Leyland Tiger chassis and had the entrance door forward of the front axle. Another body that was designed to fit underfloor engines was the Ambassador, which could be fitted to AEC, Dennis or Guy chassis. The entrance door of this was positioned halfway along its length.

The Vega was also introduced during the same period but this was designed for the more traditional front-engine vehicle. They were built on Bedford SB chassis and were designed with forward controls. This meant that the styling could undergo a radical change, with full fronts rather than half-cabs.

Although the decade started well, there were a few clouds on the horizon. Many former customers were now part of the Tilling Group, whose members had to purchase new vehicles from other members of the group – Bristol chassis had to bear ECW bodies. There was also a dispute with the trade unions that culminated in a thirty-six-week strike that saw other customers turn to rival manufacturers.

The company relocated some of its production to Loughborough when it purchased the local coachbuilding firm of W. S. Yeates. They also purchased Nudd Brothers and Lockyer Ltd, another coachbuilder, of Kegworth. These factories were then operated under the name of Duple Motor Bodies (Midland) Ltd. Duple

An example of a Duple Ambassador coach owned by Southdown. Seen here is a 1950 C26C, with sliding roof, registration number LCD 202. It was built on a Leyland Royal Tiger chassis. In 1956 the fleet number was changed from 202 to 1802.

A 1953 version of a Coronation Ambassador, again built on a Leyland Tiger chassis, but capable of seating forty-one rather than the twenty-six of its predecessor.

One of their less successful designs was this 1965 Duple Firefly on a Bedford chassis. It was owned by West Riding Coaches.

took over another coachbuilders, Willowbrook, in 1958, although the business carried on trading as a separate entity.

New designs continued to be introduced throughout the 1950s, with the Elizabethan and the Britannia for underfloor-engine chassis. These were built on heavyweight Leyland and AEC chassis and still featured a centrally placed passenger door.

At Loughborough a dual-purpose body called the Donnington was produced to fit an AEC Reliance or Leyland Tiger Cub chassis. This had the passenger door positioned forward of the front axle.

Bedford chassis had their own bodies known as the Super Vista and Super Vega. 1957 saw the introduction of the Alpine body. This was based on the Super Vega but gave passengers better vision by the inclusion of quarter lights.

In 1958 Ford produced a chassis as a rival to the Bedford SB. Duple produced a body called the Yeoman to fit this. Although produced by Ford, the vehicles were badged as 'Thames', which was Ford's commercial arm.

In 1960, the company stretched its empire further north when it took over H. V. Burlingham Ltd. of Blackpool. They had been responsible for producing a 'Seagull' range of coach bodies. It carried on trading under that name until 1962, when it became Duple Motor Bodies (Northern) Ltd. Two unsuccessful bodies were built there – the Firefly and the Dragonfly. Only six examples of the

Bere Regis & District owned this AEC Reliance fitted with a Duple Continental body introduced in 1962.

Dragonfly were ever built. These were followed by the Gannet, which was the last body to carry the Burlingham name.

In 1961 regulations were again relaxed and chassis were allowed to be increased to dimensions of 36 feet by 8 feet 2.5 inches. Chassis manufacturers, including Bedford, took advantage and introduced a VAS chassis built to the new larger dimensions. Duple came up with a brand-new design – the Continental – to fit the chassis.

Upgrades and new designs were produced throughout the 1960s, including the Bella Vista, Bella Vega, Commander, Viceroy and the Vega Major that fitted on to a six-wheeled chassis.

The Viceroy lost many of the curves of previous models, having flat sides and a straight waistline. One striking feature was the forward-leaning window pillar over the front wheels. Adverts for the vehicle also boasted fluorescent lighting, larger windows and luxurious seating. A small destination screen was incorporated centrally over the windscreen for vehicles used on long-distance service routes. Although they were relatively successful, they were not as popular as Plaxton's Panoramas and production ceased in 1972.

Bodies fitted to Ford chassis were given their own names – although they were remarkably similar to other bodies. The Trooper was based on the Bella Vega, whereas the Marauder looked very much like a Commodore.

This was Duple's fifty-two-seat Viceroy body, dating to 1967 and mounted on a Bedford VAL chassis. It belonged to Creamline Coaches of Bordon, Hampshire.

Towards the end of the 1960s, production became more concentrated at Blackpool and the Hendon premises finally closed in 1970. Willowbrook carried on trading until 1971, when it was sold to George Hughes.

In 1972 the company changed hands, being sold to the Cranleigh Group. Herbert White, the founder, died in 1973, aged 94. The 1970s saw the introduction of the Dominant series. This made its debut at the 1972 Commercial Motor Show. It had a similar style to the Plaxton Supreme range and these two were faced with very little competition. The National Bus Company purchased many Dominant bodies built onto Leyland Leopard chassis and used them on their many express routes. W. Alexander, part of the Scottish Bus Group, also bought them in large numbers. Operators received a grant to help with the cost of new service vehicles but, to receive this money, the vehicles had to comply to certain standards, one of which was wider doors than the standard coach. The body was redesigned to include a wider entrance that included double doors.

1980 saw the introduction of the new Transport Act that deregulated coach services over 30 miles. Many of these routes were run on motorways and these high mileage, faster runs favoured the more reliable, heavier chassis that AEC and Leyland produced, and so the lighter chassis produced by both Bedford and Ford went into decline. Duple's output fell from 1,000 bodies in 1976 to 500 in 1981.

Plaxton were constantly updating their range and, not wishing to be left behind, Duple employed an Italian designer, Giovanni Michelotti to update the Dominant. The Dominant 2, as it was called, had, among other modifications, a redesigned front and rear with a deeper windscreen that lined up with the bottom of the trim running beneath the side windows. The twin round headlights were replaced with rectangular units.

The 1980s saw the Dominant 3 launched. This had much smaller side windows, with very forward-sloping window pillars. A fourth version of the Dominant appeared and this reverted to rectangular windows, although they were not as deep as on the Dominant 2. They were to be found on many chassis, including Bedford, Ford, Leyland and Volvo. A high-floor version of these was also produced and this was christened the Goldliner. A Super Goldliner followed and this was fitted to a Dennis Falcon chassis, as specified by National Express, who ordered the vehicles. The last Dominants to be built were made in 1983.

Duple were now having to compete with imports from Neoplan, Van Hool and Bova, who were increasing their market share, and production dropped to just 340 bodies in 1983. Duple did co-operate with Bova, however, and produced the Calypso, an 11-m coach. This collaboration only lasted until 1984 when Bova produced their own Futura LTC body.

More designs followed with the Calypso, Carribean and Laser, but these had to compete with new imported bodies.

In June of that year Duples was sold to the Hestair Group, who already owned Dennis. The company became Hestair Duple, but the new owners could not turn the company's fortunes around.

It was not helped in 1985 when Ford announced that it was pulling out of PSV production. This was due to falling sales, as buyers preferred longer, more powerful vehicles to the lightweight range they were producing.

Revamps to the Laser and Caribbean were short-lived and, by the end of 1985, two new designs were introduced. These carried the bland names of 320 and 340, which simply referred to their height. They were available on Leyland Tiger, Volvo and DAF chassis. The 320 was also available on Bedford and Scania chassis.

A totally new design was then introduced, known as the 425. This was very aerodynamic, with the top part of the windscreen sloping backwards. Customers had the choice of a DAF or Cummins engine to power their new steed – both mounted at the rear.

Bus services were deregulated in 1986, and bus companies were facing an uncertain future and were not keen to invest in new vehicles. Dennis, however, produced the Dart in 1988 and Duple designed a body to fit it.

That year saw Hestair sell both Dennis and Duple to a management buyout and it was renamed Duple International. It was thought that this management team, with much coaching experience, could reverse the company's fortunes. This was not to be. Large potential customers like National Express preferred Plaxton's offerings and their design for the Dennis Dart buses had needed to have alterations made; consequently many fleet owners turned to Wrights and Alexanders for their bodies. A decision to close Duple was made in 1989. Plaxton purchased Duple Services Ltd, which serviced and repaired existing vehicles, and the designs for the Dart bodies were sold to Carlyle Works.

Eastern Coach Works

Although Eastern Coach Works were responsible for building far more bus bodies than luxury coaches, they deserve a chapter in this book, as they built a number of vehicles that operated long-distance coach services.

ECW can trace its history back to April 1912 when United Services Ltd was formed by three directors – Ernest Hutchinson, Andrew Alexander and John Arnold. It was formed in order to run bus services and started operating with two second-hand Commer charabancs from a garage on Horn Hill, Lowestoft.

The following year, they bought out their only local competition, who were the Great Eastern Railway, which had been operating three Milnes Daimler double-deckers.

Rapid expansion continued and they opened garages at Bishop Aukland and Durham, with a combined fleet numbering twenty-seven vehicles. The outbreak of the First World War put an end to any further expansion, as over half their

VV 7254 was a 1938 Bristol L59 with ECW bodywork. It was one of forty-nine supplied to United Counties, who kept the bus until 1955.

fleet was requisitioned by the military. The vehicles with which they were left had to be converted to coal gas or paraffin, due to the shortage of petrol.

At the end of hostilities, the company decided to expand into the coachbuilding business and new premises were obtained in Laundry Lane, Lowestoft. The first body to be built was in 1930; it was fitted to a Daimler chassis and given the fleet number B11. In the years following the First World War, there were numerous military lorry chassis abandoned in France or Belgium, and many of these were bought back by the company where they had bus bodies fitted to them. Many of these chassis were AEC Y types or Daimler CB vehicles.

At the 1921 Motor Show at Olympia, the company exhibited a new twenty-one to twenty-four seat body known as the Norfolk. These could be fitted to a number of chassis including AEC, Daimler, Ford and Guy.

For three years the entire factory's output had been used to body the company's own vehicles, but in 1924 an order for sixteen bodies were fitted to AEC chassis for Sunderland District Electric Tramways Ltd. Great Yarmouth Corporation also placed an order for seven bodies to be fitted to Guy chassis.

The company continued to expand its service operations northwards by buying out many smaller operators. This expansion came to the attention of rivals and in 1929 United Services Ltd was the subject of a successful takeover bid by Tilling & British Automobile Traction (TBAT) and the London & North Eastern Railway (LNER). TBAT was an organisation set up by Thomas Tilling Ltd and the British Electric Traction Company Ltd (BET). United was split into the Lincolnshire Road Car Company and Eastern Counties Omnibus Company (ECOC). The body-building factory in Laundry Lane became part of the latter. As it was now part of the Tilling Group, this opened up new markets, but they were restricted to building bodies for companies within the group, although they were allowed to fulfil orders already taken. This included an order for double-deckers for Lowestoft Transport and Great Yarmouth Corporation Transport, using AEC Regent chassis. One of the eight buses for Lowestoft was fitted with a diesel, rather than petrol, engine and this was the first recorded diesel to have been fitted with a body at the factory. The order was to replace trams in the town.

Over the next four years, orders were fulfilled from Southern Vectis and East Kent in the south to Yorkshire Traction and Caledonian in the north.

The company managed to survive the 1930s slump. One of the reasons for this was that they standardised their products, thus reducing costs. Many of their bodies were fitted to Leyland chassis but, as the decade progressed, more and more Bristol chassis were used. The Bristol Tramway & Carriage Company was also part of the Tilling Group. Although there was initially some customer resistance to Bristol chassis, the combination gradually received favour and many thousands of such vehicles were produced over many years.

In 1935 the first combination of a Gardner diesel engine was used to power a Bristol chassis fitted with ECOC bodywork. This was to prove a popular combination that lasted into the 1980s. That year also saw the workforce expand to 1,000 and it was decided to split the operation into two – services and bodybuilding. Eastern Coach Works was formed in 1936 and was wholly a subsidiary of ECOC.

Up to the Second World War, single- and double-deck buses were supplied to a number of operators, including Black & White, Southern Vectis, Western Welsh and Brighton & Hove. Three open-toppers were also supplied to Westcliffe-on-Sea Motor Services. New bodies were also fitted to old chassis for other operators.

Although the war did not halt bus production, it was forced to continue elsewhere. Being situated on the coast, it was feared that the factory would fall into enemy hands should there be an invasion, so alternative premises had to be found. Over 100 bombs were dropped on the town but their premises escaped serious damage. The new factory was at Lithlingborough, Northamptonshire, in a bus depot once used by Wellingborough Motor Services.

One of the wartime tasks undertaken by the factory was to convert some buses to use gas as fuel. They also had to manufacture kits that would convert single-deck buses to ambulances. The seating arrangements on some vehicles were also altered to accommodate as many passengers as possible.

As the threat of invasion decreased, the company was allowed to return to their original premises and production restarted on a limited scale. At the end of hostilities, many of the staff that had relocated to Lithlingborough returned to Lowestoft. Production did continue at the Northamptonshire plant using local labour until 1951 when the premises were sold.

Peacetime brought an increase in orders, but a shortage of some materials meant that meeting the demand was difficult.

Bournemouth was the destination of this 1951 Bristol with ECW C35F coachwork. KRU 997 spent its whole life with Hants & Dorset, before being withdrawn in 1967.

Another example of a 1951 Bristol with ECW bodywork. This vehicle, which started life working for the Southern National Omnibus Co. Ltd, could seat thirty-seven passengers. It was sold to Rodgers of Redcar in 1966.

A 1954 Bristol SCX6P with ECW B35F bodywork. Eastern National purchased the bus new and kept it for ten years, before selling it to Vaggs Coaches Ltd of Knockin Heath. It was disposed of in 1967.

By the end of 1946 a total of 5,000 bodies had been made at the factory since it was built. A limited number of body designs were available and, being owned by Tillings, it made good business sense to use chassis supplied by Bristol, as they were also part of the Tilling group.

In 1948, Tillings was nationalised, becoming part of the British Transport Commission (BTC). This was set up by the Labour government as part of an integrated transport system that covered road, rail and sea. The company was only allowed to fulfil orders from within the group, although orders already received could be honoured.

Restrictions on the size of buses meant that, prior to 1948, buses measuring 8-foot wide could only be used on certain roads. Changes to these regulations came in 1950 when the restrictions to 8-foot vehicles were relaxed. The maximum length for a single-decker of 27 feet and 6 inches was also increased to 30 feet, while a double-deck bus with two rear axles could be lengthened from 26 feet to 27 feet. Further relaxation of rules were introduced in 1956 when twin-axled doubles could be 30-feet long, and in 1962 singles could be built 36-feet long. The width of vehicles could also be increased to 8 feet and 2.5 inches.

In 1950 a new coach design was introduced. This differed from previous designs as it was not derived from a bus design. It was a full-fronted body made to fit onto a Bristol L6B chassis. Some later bodies were also fitted to Leyland and AEC chassis.

This 1957 Eastern Counties Bristol started its career with United Counties. It changed hands in 1962 and stayed with Eastern National until 1971, when it moved to Morris Bros of Swansea.

A 1957 thirty-nine-seat ECW-bodied Bristol LS, owned by Eastern Counties and seen at Victoria.

A similar Bristol to the top photo, but with differences to the radiator grill and window above the driver's seat. 280 NHK was owned from new in 1959 by Eastern National until late 1970, when it was sold to Progressive Coaches.

Another design for a single-deck was introduced in 1957. This was designated as MW (medium weight) and could be used as a bus, dual-purpose vehicle or coach. This was superseded in 1961 by a new MW design. 2,000 of these were made by 1967 when production ended.

In 1954 a new smaller design was also introduced. Known as the SC (small capacity), 320 were made over an eight-year production run. 1959 saw a replacement for the SC introduced. This was the SU (small underfloor). Two versions were available – the SUS being 24 feet and 4 inches, and the SUL measuring 28 feet. Only the SUL could be supplied with a coach body.

During 1962 the RE (rear engine) was introduced. They were made in three lengths: RES (32 feet, 6 inches), REL (36 feet) and REM (39 feet). Bus, dual-purpose or coach bodies could be fitted to all three. Coach bodies were fitted to chassis with higher frames than for bus bodies. Production finished in 1975.

In 1975 the government announced that Leyland Motors would acquire a 25 per cent stake in ECW. This meant that the company was no longer restricted to supplying vehicles to other nationalised companies and their bodies could be fitted to Leyland and Daimler chassis.

During the 1960s much production centred on Leyland Atlanteans and Bristol VRs, which were a replacement for the successful Bristol Lodekka.

A 1964 Bristol MW69 with ECW C39F bodywork. It spent its entire life with Eastern National, before being withdrawn in October 1979.

In 1968, a new Sabre design was displayed at the Commercial Motor Show. It was mounted on an AEC chassis. It did not impress the public or operators. No orders were placed and it never went into production.

1969 saw British Leyland, as it had become, increase its stake to 50 per cent, not only in ECW but also in Bristol. The other 50 per cent was owned by the National Bus Company. A new company was formed – Leyland National Ltd – which was a joint venture between the British Leyland and the National Bus Company. It was founded to build buses at a new plant at Workington in Cumberland. This plant would have grave consequences to ECW. The Leyland Atlanteans and Nationals built there were serious competition for the Bristol VRs and REs being built at Lowestoft.

Production continued into the 1970s, however. A new forty-nine-seater was introduced in 1972 for use with Bristol or Leyland chassis. Between 1972 and 1975, 2,000 vehicles were built.

1981 saw another design, the B51, unveiled. It was designed to fit on to a Bristol RELH chassis. It was soon decided, however, that it should be made to fit on to a Leyland Leopard chassis and the body was modified to do so. A modified design was made to fit the Leyland Tiger chassis. This longer body started to suffer structural failures, and kits had to be supplied to operators to strengthen the bodies.

Originally owned by Wilts & Dorset, this thirty-nine-seat Bristol MW6G with ECW bodywork was sold in October 1972 to Hants & Dorset, who operated it for four years. The vehicle has now been privately preserved.

In 1982 the NBC announced that it had sold its share of Bus Manufacturers (Holdings) Ltd to Leyland, which meant that, for the first time, Leyland had complete control of ECW and Bristol Motors. Another problem for the industry was that the government announced the ending of the 50 per cent grant that was available to operators buying new vehicles. This, of course, led to a downturn in orders.

ECW had problems with the unions over proposed new working practices and, coupled with a falling order book, it meant that the good times were over at the Lowestoft plant. By 1983, only five bodies per week were being produced.

That year did not start well either when Bristol Motors announced its closure in January. The following month ninety-eight of Eastern Coach Work's 500-strong workforce were made redundant.

A rare high spot occurred in 1984 when a new vehicle was displayed at the Commercial Motor Show. It was an ECW-bodied luxury double-deck coach owned by Ebdons of Kent. It was awarded the Gold Cup. The Silver Cup went to a Leyland DAB midibus. That year also saw the factory supplying parts to be fitted to vehicles being assembled at other plants.

In 1985 the company staged a charity open day in support of a CT scanner for the local hospital. £3,500 was raised. Many older, preserved vehicles returned to the factory to take part in the event.

A new spray plant was installed at the premises later that year, which boded well for the future. The following year, however, Leyland Motors was the subject of a management buyout and the Lowestoft plant was not part of the deal.

1986 saw production fall to 1,000 vehicles. This compared to 2,400 only six years earlier. ECW looked abroad to fill their order books and were fairly successful, with orders from Greece, Hong Kong and America being won.

The last order at the plant was for London Transport Olympians and when this order was completed in January 1987, the factory closed. The factory was demolished soon after and the site redeveloped.

Harringtons

Like many coachbuilders, Harringtons can trace their roots back over 100 years. It was in 1897 that Thomas Harrington started to build a variety of horse-drawn wagons in his workshops situated in Church Street, Brighton. Within three years, his business had grown so big that he needed to open showrooms in King Street. By now, the motor car was becoming more popular and he concentrated more and more of his efforts into building car and commercial vehicle bodies.

It was not long before many car manufacturers were building their own standardised bodies for mass-produced motors but, at the more exclusive end of the market, bodies were still built by privately owned coachbuilders and this was where Harringtons concentrated their efforts. Their reputation for building luxury vehicles put them in good stead when they ventured into the luxury coach market.

To carry out this new work, they opened a new workshop in Old Shoreham Road, Hove. Choosing this site was to have repercussions, as there was no room to expand, being hemmed in by a railway, main road and cemetery. Production was steady, with the weekly production limited to around four vehicles per week due to space considerations.

As with many companies, the Second World War put an end to all normal production and the factory was turned over to helping in the war effort, with the factory making or repairing military vehicles, and making aircraft components such as frames.

After the war, the company used some of the knowledge gained in aircraft production in the manufacture of coach bodies. Another revolutionary discovery of the 1950s was fibreglass, and Harrington's used this for the more complicated panel shapes. Due to the risk of fire or even explosion in the production process, the panels were produced in separate premises within the site. They had produced a new coach body – the Cavalier – and the success of this design was putting a strain on production on the limited site.

The company had managed to remain a family-run firm with the founder's two sons, Thomas and Ernest, together with other family members joining the board

Southdown 1178, a 1937 Leyland Tiger PS7 with Harrington C32R body fitted with folding roof, is seen here touting for business on Brighton prom.

This was one of only six examples of a 1947 Leyland Tiger PS1 to receive a Harrington C32F body. It was fitted with a full-width canopy and stayed in service with Southdown until 1957. It carried the fleet number 1266.

Photographed in Buxton was this 1957 Harrington-bodied Leyland Tiger Cub. It belonged to Gliderways of Smethwick.

but, in 1961, the Robins & Day group, which was owned by Rootes, purchased a stake in Harringtons.

The 1960s saw the company return to its roots in making car bodies, and it started making fibreglass hard tops for sports cars, including the Sunbeam Alpine and Triumph TR4 made by the Rootes Group. Harringtons had been a Rootes agent since the 1930s and they had car showrooms in Hove and Worthing. Rootes were trying to get into the upper ends of the car market and entered Le Mans with a closed-body Alpine. It was thought that success here would lead to increased sales, with Harringtons making the bodies. Unfortunately the perceived increase in sales never materialised and Rootes's fortunes began to founder. The Alpine coupe was dropped from the range in 1963.

There were not enough profits being made from coach production and not enough finance available to make replacements for the Grenadier and Cavalier ranges. Being a smaller bespoke manufacturer was no longer cost effective and they could not compete with the larger manufacturers.

The last coach to be made was a Grenadier in 1966. This was registered to Greenslades Tours of Exeter, with a registration number FFJ 13D. The factory was subsequently used as a vehicle service centre by British Telecom, before being demolished in 1999.

Southdown took delivery of this Harrington Wayfarer-bodied Leyland Royal Tiger in 1951. It originally carried the fleet number 829 before becoming 1829 and then 1689 inn 1961. Photographed on Madiera Drive Brighton.

A 1933 AEC Regal with Harrington's bodywork, belonging to Yeoman Coaches.

This AEC Reliance with a Harrington Cavalier body was delivered new to Yelloway in 1965, before being sold to Rosemary Coaches of Kings Lynn.

Plaxton

Plaxton's were founded by Frederick William Plaxton of Scarborough in 1907, when he opened a joinery workshop. He soon expanded into the building trade, becoming responsible for building the town's futurist cinema. During the Second World War, he started to manufacture shell boxes and wooden aircraft parts from the Olympia Skating Rink on Scarborough's Foreshore.

Although a fire in 1943 destroyed the company's records, it is known that in the 1920s he made his first foray into coachbuilding when he constructed a charabanc body to fit on to a Model T Ford chassis.

During the 1920s, however, he concentrated his efforts on building bodies for cars and soon became known for the quality of his products. Using Crossley chassis, he was even engaged to build cars for royalty, including cars for the princes of Wales and York to use on foreign tours of Australia and South Africa respectively. He also built a limousine for King George V.

He still found time to produce charabanc bodies for local operators throughout the 1920s and exhibited at the Olympia Motor Show, where he gained second prize.

In the mid-1930s, he expanded his operation with the construction of new workshops. This led to an increase in production, and coaches with his bodywork began to be a regular sight outside his native county of Yorkshire.

It was becoming common practice for operators to update their fleets by fitting new bodies to existing chassis and Plaxton's fitted quite a number for Lancashire

Percival's Coaches of Richmond purchased this Leyland Comet CPO1 second-hand in September 1957 and sold it again in 1964.

WH Patch of Stamford FCT320 operated this 1951 Plaxton-bodied Commer Avenger I.

Motor Traders. New chassis made by AEC, Leyland and Bedford also received new bodies made by the company.

The Second World War brought an abrupt end to coachbuilding and the factory was used entirely for the production of munitions. They also produced engine casings for Rolls Royce and Bristol aero engines. In 1943 a fire destroyed the factory. A Mr Quarton came to the rescue, with the loan of some premises in which to continue production. He was rewarded with a directorship of the company, which he kept until he retired in 1979.

After the end of hostilities, the company was not slow in returning to building coach bodies, and the first vehicle made was in early 1946. Bedford, Commer and Austin were the main manufacturers of smaller chassis and were used for 27–29 seat bodies, whereas the larger thirty-three-seat chassis were mainly produced by Leyland and AEC. Other suppliers included Foden, Albion, Crossley and Dennis. Plaxton's bodies only needed minor alterations to fit onto the different chassis.

In 1951 Plaxton's became a limited company and expanded into making bodies for fire engines for the Ministry of Works. These became known as Green Goddesses. In the late 1950s they also built over seventy mobile canteens and general-purpose vans for USAF personnel stationed in the UK.

Returning to coach production, one of the major advances in chassis design of the 1950s was the placing of engines underneath the floor. The company's market share increased throughout the decade and this was helped by Bedfords. Until 1954 they had exclusively used Duple bodywork in their advertising material, but in a change of policy they also showed their chassis with Plaxton bodywork.

This is a Plaxton Venturer body on an AEC chassis, delivered to Silcox Coaches in the early 1950s.

Another Plaxton Venturer body, mounted on an AEC chassis, this time delivered to Hanson Coaches.

This boosted sales to the smaller operators throughout the country. The company was not only able to produce 'off the peg' bodies like the Consort and Venturer, but it could provide bodies to customers' requirements. The 1950s also saw the end of bulkheads separating the driver from his passengers and all new vehicles were forward-control designs. This change to full fronts from half-cabs also led to radiators being hidden, and new designs of radiator grille being introduced. The decade also saw a relaxation in chassis specifications and an increase in size, from 27 feet by 7 feet and 6 inches to 30 feet by 8 feet, was allowed.

Following the death of Frederick, the founder, in 1957, his son took over the running of the business. With other members of the board, a decision was taken to build new premises at Eastfield, just outside Scarborough. This opened in 1961.

In 1961 the maximum length of 30 feet was increased to 36 feet, with an increase in overall width to 8 feet and 2.5 inches being allowed. The first example Plaxton produced using these new dimensions was a Panorama-bodied AEC Reliance built for Sheffield United Tours. Leyland were soon to produce a lengthened version of the Leopard.

In 1962 Bedford produced a new 36-foot chassis with twin-axled steering. This was called the Val. Plaxton's first body design for this new chassis was an Embassy forty-six-seater, which was shown at the Commercial Motor Show in 1962, but work was put in hand to produce a Panorama body to fit as soon as possible.

Another design feature of the period was one-piece wrap-around windscreens. The same glass was also used on the rear of the Panoramas. These one-piece screens were prone to failure, especially on high-speed motorway runs, and it was not long until two separate screens were reintroduced.

The company were also building bus bodies by this time, but a new Panorama was to revolutionise design in the 1960s. This design gave the passengers a better view of the passing scenery by decreasing the number of window pillars, resulting in fewer, longer and deeper windows. Curved glass had been used either side of flat windscreens but, as the decade progressed, the windscreens became curved and wider, and the separate windows on the front corners began to disappear. These wrap-around windscreens echoed the designs being used on private cars like the Vauxhall Cresta.

In 1963 a smaller rival, W. L. Thurgood of Hertfordshire, ceased trading. Plaxton's took over their premises to act as a service and repair centre in the southern part of the country.

In 1964 a Panorama with a newly designed front was shown at the Commercial Motor Show. 1968 saw the introduction of the Panorama Elite, in which the most noticeable difference was that the side windows curved inwards at the top.

The 1970s saw more expansion, due partly to their new premises at Eastfield being far superior to their rivals still trying to adapt older premises. 1970 saw the production of over 1,000 new bodies. Midland Red became a major customer in 1971, ordering 100 bus bodies to fit onto Ford R192 chassis. A further forty were added to this order.

1973 saw production grow to 1,300 bodies, which was about a third of the total national production of single-deck bus/coach bodies that year.

It is perhaps surprising that, until the 1970s, timber had still been a major component in building the frames for bodies to fit on to, but the mid-1970s saw a shift to all-metal bodies using steel frameworks. 1974 saw the introduction of the Supreme, which used more metal in its construction and side windows with more pronounced curves than the Elite it replaced.

The late 1970s also saw a change in body shapes. Continental designs had started to use high-floor bodies, and Plaxton's designed their own Viewmaster body to keep up with modern trends, and one example was displayed at the 1978 Motor Show at Birmingham.

In 1979 a new, smaller design was introduced to fit on to a Bedford CF light van chassis. This could seat seventeen to twenty passengers.

The 1980s saw the introduction of the Paramount body. This was easily recognised by the window behind the entrance door sloping upwards towards the higher floor. This higher floor level also increased the luggage capacity beneath the floor.

In 2005 Plaxton became part of the Alexander Dennis group and is continuing to produce high-quality coach bodies.

Minster Coaches owned this Commer Avenger, fitted with Plaxton Venturer coachwork.

Pete's of Evesham owned this Bedford J2 with Plaxton Consort bodywork.

This is a 1972 Bedford Val with Plaxton Panorama Elite bodywork, operated by Dewsway Coaches.

Wallace Arnold favoured Volvo power for their Plaxton Paramount-bodied coaches. This one was photographed in Torquay.

Comparisons of Leyland Tigers with Plaxton Paramount bodies can be made here, as two National Express coaches, which were run by Shamrock & Rambler, stand side by side. On the left is the 1983 A104 HNC, standing beside WOC 728T of 1979 vintage.

Chapter 5

The Operators

Bristol Greyhound

Greyhound Buses was founded in 1921 to run bus services in Bristol. Four years later it started a service to London, picking up at several points on the way. This journey took eight hours. Expansion saw services from Bristol to Bournemouth and Paignton, as well as a service from the capital to Bournemouth.

In 1928 it was taken over by Bristol Tramways, who had been operating services within the city, but it continued to operate under the Greyhound name.

It operated express coach services until 1972, when it was taken over by the National Bus Company and forced to use the new owner's livery. In 1988 it became part of Arriva, who reintroduced the Greyhound brand.

This Bristol LS6B with thirty-nine-seat ECW bodywork was delivered to Bristol Tramways in 1953. It originally bore the fleet number 2865 before becoming 2087 in March 1961. It became part of the Bristol Omnibus Company fleet in 1957, where it served until 1965 and was eventually sold for scrap in 1973.

Two Bristol coaches with ECW bodies, with the 1966 body below looking far more modern than the 1965 version above.

Epsom Coaches

In 1920 Roddy Richmond went into business with his brother-in-law, Jim Reeves. They acquired premises behind the shops in the high street, with a garage large enough to house two vehicles, as well as an even larger barn-like structure.

Like many young entrepreneurs after the First World War, they took advantage of many surplus vehicles being sold off by the War Department, converting them to charabancs.

Their first purchase was a Lancia chassis bought for £200, which needed a further £300 spent on it. A new body cost £386, making a total outlay of just under £900. Further purchases followed and, by 1925, they owned a Model T Ford, three Lancias and three Thorneycrofts. Other makes followed, including Strakers Squires, AECs and Crossleys. They were used to take racegoers to regular meetings at tracks in Kent and Sussex. They were also used by Epsom Football Club to take players and fans to away matches. Servicemen recovering in local hospitals also used them for day trips to London and surrounding areas.

They bought their first saloon coach in 1929. This was a thirty-two-seat Albion chassis, with a London Lorries – soon to become Duple – body. Another Albion, a Gilford and five smaller Bedfords soon followed.

One of the company's first vehicles was this Model T Ford, bought in 1921 and capable of carrying fourteen passengers.

1928 saw the purchase of PK1815, a saloon on a Reo Chassis.

In 1930, they obtained express licenses and were able to start daily trips to Brighton and Worthing (22½p single, 25p return) as well as twice-weekly trips to Bognor and Southsea.

Customers hiring charabancs were not allowed publicly to advertise their trips if they were charging for seats, but clubs and societies were allowed to use newsletters to inform members of forthcoming outings.

In 1934 the firm were forced to move from their premises, as the high street in Epsom was being widened. They found new premises in South Street.

At the outbreak of the Second World War, the War Department requisitioned five of their six coaches, as well as six horseboxes they also owned. His one coach was put to good use, however, ferrying schoolchildren to schools, workmen to bombsites, wounded soldiers to hospitals and even German POWs to work. The coach windows were removed on safety grounds.

In 1944, they managed to buy another new coach, a thirty-two-seat Bedford Utility with wooden seats.

Roddy's health had deteriorated by the end of hostilities and he would have liked to retire, but his eldest son, Jack, who had been a bomber pilot, had been tragically killed on a bombing mission. His younger son, Roy, was still serving in Egypt, so he was forced to carry on. It was 1947 until he left the forces and decided to return to the family business.

Fuel for excursions was rationed after the war, but this did not extend to regular services, and weekly trips to Brighton and Southsea were restarted.

Epsom's were one of the better firms to work for. They never laid off their staff during the winter months – in return, they were amenable to taking on other

By 1932 coach design had become more conventional, as this Duple body on a Gilford chassis illustrates.

work and spent much of the off-peak season helping mechanics maintain the coaches, so that the fleet would be in tip-top condition at the start of the summer season.

In the 1950s, they took over Bookham's Coaches and E. E. Law of Leatherhead. One of the latter's contracts was a regular trip to Montreux. Roddy was loth to send his coaches abroad, as breakdowns on the continent could be costly, but his son, Roy persuaded him to honour the contract.

By the late fifties, the services to the coast had expanded to include Eastbourne, Hastings and Bournemouth on the south coast, as well as Leigh-on-Sea and Southend-on-Sea in Essex. The range of excursions had grown as well to take in Cheddar Gorge, Salisbury, and Stonehenge.

In the 1960s holiday tours were being arranged wherein groups of pensioners were taken to Margate for a week, with day trips from the resort to surrounding attractions arranged in the package. Day trips to the continent were also becoming popular. Passports were not needed for these outings, which left from Lydd Airport to Le Touquet or by ferry from Dover to Calais.

At around the same time, the company wanted to run local bus services in competition with London Transport, but the traffic commissioners would not grant them a licence. A neat solution was to form a club. Anyone wishing to make use of the service had to join a club at an annual fee of 2s 6d and then they

A new 1950 AEC Regal III, sporting a Whitson body, poses at Epsom.

could be charged a fare for their journey. The first service ran between Tattenham Corner and Epsom Station.

The Road Traffic Acts of the 1930s meant that any bus or coach operator within the Metropolitan Police Area had to be granted a licence from the traffic commissioners to be able to run an excursion or route, and they were not very forthcoming with these licenses. The London General Omnibus Co. were exempt from these regulations. The Metropolitan Police Area stretched for 30 miles from the centre of London. If an excursion left this area, a backing licence was required from one of the surrounding traffic areas, such as South Eastern, West Midlands, Yorkshire, to name a few. These excursions had to be advertised in 'Notices and Proceedings', whereby the applications could be challenged. These Ns & Ps still exist for stage-carriage routes, whereby any applications for alterations to bus services must be advertised forty-two days before commencement of the service. These can be found on VOSA's website. This red tape strangled many small companies and led to monopolies operating all the major routes from Victoria and other coach stations. These groups included British Electric Traction (BET) and Thomas Tilling in their number.

Applications by Epsom Coaches were routinely opposed by the large companies in their area, including Southdown, East Kent Road Car Company and Maidstone & District, as well as British Railways. Adequate services existed or unfair competition was cited as the reasons for objections. Expensive legal representation had to be employed to present new applications to traffic commissioners, who had to be convinced that there was a public need for a new service. For many smaller concerns this was an expense they were not prepared to risk. Smaller local companies were also prone to oppose their local rival's applications.

Epsom Coaches had a very limited number of points where they could pick up their passengers and any increase was strongly opposed. On top of that, any licences they did have had to be renewed every three years and this was again an expensive and time-consuming process.

They were not without some successes, however, and they were granted licences to run to Eastbourne and Hastings. As the 1950s passed by, people became more affluent and purchased their own family transport, putting pressure on the coach operators, who were losing excursion traffic to the motor car. Some of Epsom's local rivals in Kingston and Sutton ceased trading, and Epsom Coaches were successful in adding their pick-up points to those they already had.

In the 1970s foreign package tours took off and tour operators needed coach companies to take holidaymakers to airports. As this travel was included in the overall price, a road service licence was needed for each route. Epsoms applied for and won a route to Manston Airport in Kent, despite opposition from the East Kent Road Car Company.

The company also opened booking offices in Leatherhead and Banstead, as well as Epsom, and became agents for other coach operators including Southdown and Wallace Arnold.

The advent of roll on/roll off ferries made continental days trips more practicable and these proved popular. They even reached as far as East Germany and Poland when they were hired by the Wimbledon Speedway Supporters Club to attend away meetings.

One area of the business that went into decline, however, was taking workers to large factories. On a daily basis, four coaches had been needed for Wildts of Great Bookham and three for the workers at Gala Cosmetics. The reasons for their demise were twofold – more workers could afford cars and the output of factories was generally shrinking.

On 31 July 1969, Roddy, the founder of the business, sadly passed away in a nursing home in Leatherhead.

The 1970s witnessed further expansion, with more continental tours, some even venturing behind the Iron Curtain. The size of coaches was also expanding with vehicles up to 12 metres being allowed, which was up from 30 feet (under 10 metres) when the company started. Servicing facilities had to be improved to cater for these longer vehicles.

The 1980s saw local rivals, Surrey Motors of Sutton and RACS (Duvals) of Mitcham, both cease trading and Epsom Coaches began to run some of the excursions their rivals used to operate.

The decade also saw Leyland completely redesign their chassis, the Tiger, to compete with their foreign rivals. Unfortunately many of the new components were untested and proved to be unreliable, so Epsom's turned to Volvo to supply their coaches. Some of the new vehicles (B10Ms) were put on excursions to the French Riviera and proved to be so successful that only Volvo chassis were purchased in the next ten years.

Local services were not ignored though and, in 1983, the company took on the railways by operating commuter services from the Dorking, Reigate and Tattenham Corner areas into the capital. Fares were only £1.50 for a return, which undercut the railways by £1.20. While in London, the coaches were used for excursions before operating the return trips. The service was dropped when the railways improved their services.

In 1986 the coaching business was deregulated. This came at a time when the tourist industry had been hit by Colonel Gaddafi's terrorist activities, and foreign visitors numbers, especially Americans, had plummeted. The company saw the opportunity to use the excess capacity to enter the stage-carriage business and a new commercial service, Route 5, ran on the first day of deregulation. They were also successful in winning three routes put out to tender by Surrey County Council. Although the Plaxton-bodied Leyland Leopards used for these services were reliable, they were not passenger-friendly with steep steps, narrow gangways and reclining seats and so, in 1987, the company purchased five Bedford YMT chassis with Plaxton Derwent bodies. A period of 'bus wars' ensued as the established operators did not like the new competition. This took the form of buses being blocked in at bus stops and even damage being inflicted to the vehicles.

The 1990s saw a change in allegiance to vehicle suppliers. The recession of that time made imported vehicles more expensive and tests using Dennis Javelins had proved successful – a large number were purchased between 1994 and 1999.

In 1997, an agreement was reached with London General to take over the S1 and 413 bus routes, buying eleven used Optare Metrorider vehicles. These proved to be unreliable and eleven new Dennis Mini Pointer Darts were purchased. The bus arm of the company was rebranded, with Quality Line logos being added to the livery. The Epsom Buses name was then dropped from the livery and eventually the vehicles were repainted in London Buses red livery.

The company continues to run a very successful operation. It maintains its vehicles in its own workshops and trains the majority of its own drivers.

By maintaining its high standards, it has continued to be one of the most successful privately owned bus/coach companies in the country.

Midland Red

Midland Red was the trading name of the Birmingham & Midland Motorbus Company. It was formed in 1905 by a group of businessmen to operate motor bus services in Birmingham. Insufficient interest in the new scheme led to it being taken over by British Electric Traction (BET) the following year.

The introduction of the motor bus was not exactly successful in the city and in 1907 the motor bus was ditched in favour of the old horse-drawn vehicles. It was to be 1912 before the company ventured into motorised transport again, with the purchase of some Tilling-Stevens petrol-electric buses. The fleet carried the name 'Midland' and, sporting a red livery, they soon began to be known locally as Midland Reds.

Within the city, Birmingham Corporation Tramways had used its statutory powers to acquire all the tramways. This meant that BMMO decided it would be better to concentrate its efforts on bringing passengers from the surrounding areas into the city. Depots were opened in Walsall, Hereford, Stafford, Leicester and other towns, and tram systems within the area gradually succumbed to the Midland Red bus.

In 1930 the Great Western Railway and the London, Midland & Scottish Railway acquired a 50 per cent share of the company, which meant the company became 50 per cent state-owned when the railways were nationalised.

In 1921 the firm had expanded into express coach services, starting with routes to Weston-Super-Mare and Llandudno. The Second World War put an end to these services but, after the war, the services restarted and the coming of the motorway system enabled non-stop services such as Birmingham–London and Coventry–London to be inaugurated. The Birmingham–London service was inaugurated on the opening day of the M1 in 1959, with an advertised journey time of 3 hrs 25 mins but, in practice, journey times of less than 3 hrs were often obtained. The vehicles used were C5s converted for motorway use and classified as CM5s. These had five-speed gearboxes with overdrive, which were capable of speeds of over 80 mph.

The opening of the M5 led to new services between Bristol and London, and Birmingham and Worcester.

In 1968 BET sold its share to the government, and the following year it became a subsidiary of the National Bus Company. In 1977 the company was split into smaller localised companies, including Midland Red North, Midland Fox and Midland South. These small companies were eventually taken over by Arriva, Stagecoach and First.

2277 was a 1939 vehicle, built by the BMMO with a Duple body, seen here heading for Kidderminster.

Introduced in 1949, 3303 was an underfloor-engine vehicle with Duple body. It was revolutionary when introduced, making competitors' vehicles look very dated. 1954 saw the introduction of sixty-three of these new coaches classified as C3s.

UHA 243 was bodied by Willowbrook to a Midland Red design. The class were suitable for day excursions, but not for the motorways that were opened five years after they were introduced.

Reusing the chassis with a new body is UHA 193, now sporting Plaxton coachwork fitted in 1962 after losing its original Willowbrook body.

Two views of 1965 Motorway Express coaches introduced to speed travelers from the Midlands to the capital. Built by Midland Red, these CM6Ts were capable of speeds of up to 85 mph.

2057 was a 1964 Leyland Leopard, with a Plaxton Panorama body, seen on an express service.

Another Leyland Leopard purchased in 1965, sporting a Duple Commander body.

National Express

The National Express brand was first seen in 1974. It was a result of the Transport Act 1968. The National Bus Company was formed as a holding company for many local state-owned bus companies. Many of these ran long-distance coach services. Originally they were just branded as 'National'. Although the vehicles appeared in National Express livery, they were still operated by the original companies whose names could still be seen within the livery.

This state of affairs only lasted until 1980 when the Transport Act of 1980 deregulated coach services. In 1988 it was privatised in a management buyout. 1989 continental services to Alicante, Paris and Barcelona were bought from Wallace Arnold. Services between London and Scotland were also purchased from Stagecoach.

1991 saw the sale of National Express to the Drawlane Group and the following year the National Express Group plc was floated on the Stock Exchange. The

One of National Express's older vehicles was this 1976 Leyland Leopard, with Alexander body and operated by Eastern Counties.

group's services had a virtual monopoly of long-distance coach routes throughout the country until 2007, when Megabus, which is part of the Stagecoach Group, entered the field with fares as low as £1.

Many National Express routes serve airports, including Heathrow, Gatwick, Luton, Midlands and Stansted. These routes were formally marketed as Speedlink, Jetlink, Flightlink and Airlink.

Although the vehicles are branded as 'National Express', many of the coaches are owned and operated by private operators who work the services under contract. One of the clauses stipulates that vehicles bearing National Express livery must be used or there will be a financial penalty should a vehicle in another livery have to be used. There are about thirty-four operators throughout the country who are contracted to run these services, including Yellowbus of Bournemouth in the south, through Stagecoach Yorkshire, to Parks of Hamilton in Scotland and Ulsterbus in Belfast.

Formally owned by Hants & Dorset, this Leyland Leopard with Plaxton bodywork, fleet number 3126, was now owned by Shamrock & Rambler. The twin passenger doors can be seen that would qualify it for a government grant.

Four various fronts in these two images, which show how designs changed between 1978 (above right) to 1991 (below right). Above left is a 1983 Leyland Tiger with Plaxton Paramount body. Below left is a 1990 Volvo B10M with Plaxton Expressliner body, next to a slightly newer example with revised radiator grille.

This 1997 Volvo B10M with Plaxton Premiere Expressliner II bodywork had recently changed hands from Stagecoach Cambus to Midland Red South. The sign-writing on the side still advertised Cambridge–London services, while the destination blind states Liverpool via Birmingham.

A 1984 MCW Metroliner leaving Bournemouth on its way to the capital.

Royal Blue

Royal Blue is another operator that can trace its history back to pre-motorised transport days. It was in 1880 that Thomas Elliott started a business in Bournemouth called Royal Blue & Branksome Mews. They hired out horse-drawn vehicles as well as running a blacksmiths, a saddlery and coachbuilders.

At that time the railway had not reached Bournemouth, so he saw the business opportunity of running stagecoaches from Bournemouth town centre to the nearest railway station at Holmsley on the Southampton & Dorchester Railway.

When the railway reached Bournemouth in 1888, this put an end to this service, so he diversified by running trips around Bournemouth and to the New Forest by horse-drawn vehicles and later by charabancs. Doubtless the new railway brought him many passengers for this new venture.

Thomas died in 1911 and his two sons, John and William, inherited the business.

This 1951 Bristol was fitted with ECW C37F bodywork. Its fleet number was 1313 and it survived in service until 1965. The following year it was exported to Cyprus, where it worked for another eleven years.

Royal Blue bought their first charabanc in 1913 and further purchases soon saw an end to all their horse-drawn services. In 1919, there was a railway strike and Royal Blue was not slow to see a potential for profit by running their charabancs to London. The service proved to be so successful that it carried on after the railway service resumed. In 1920 the service was increased to twice weekly and the following year to twice daily. In the 1920s, bus services were heavily regulated and it was not until 1928 that Royal Blue were granted licences to pick up and set down en route. More routes were opened, with services joining Birmingham, Bristol and Plymouth with the capital.

The Road Traffic Act of 1930 led to more regulation, and it was easier for operators to expand by purchasing rival operators than to apply for new licences. Other operators expanded by agreeing with rivals to share services and share revenues. Royal Blue did both and acquired Traveller Coaches of Plymouth and Olympic Services of Portsmouth, while entering into joint agreements with Southdown, East Kent, Greyhound and others. In 1934 they were one of the founders of Associated Motorways, which co-ordinated routes of six large operators.

In 1934 the Elliott brothers sold the business to Western National and Southern National, which were part of the Tilling Group. One of the outcomes from this change of ownership was that further new vehicles were bought from Bristols, which were also owned by Tillings.

The Second World War saw an end to Royal Blue's services for about four years, due to fuel shortages and bomb damage to their garages.

In 1947 it sold its bus operation to the British Transport Commission, but services continued to expand even under state control. There were still fuel shortages, but this applied to private motorists as well so many chose to make longer journeys by coach rather than private car. The closure of many railway branch lines also put more traffic on to the roads and 1965 proved to be Royal Blue's busiest year, with over 1.5 million passengers using their services.

1963 saw the creation of the state-owned Transport Holding Company, which in 1969 became the National Bus Company, of which Royal Blue remained a part. Another change occurred in 1972 when the NBC formed National Travel, which became National Express, whose remit was to run long-distance coach services. Royal Blue's name was obtained, even though it was to be seen on National Express's white livery.

In 1980 coach services were deregulated and in 1983 Western National was divided into four companies, which were subsequently privatised. In 1986 National Express stopped using the names of regional operators from its coaches and Royal Blue disappeared after 106 years.

This Bristol with ECW bodywork entered service in 1952. It was fleet number 1286. It served with Western National and Southern National until 1968. It has now been preserved.

This 1953 Southern National Bristol LS6G with ECW C39F coachwork had the fleet number 1295. It served with Southern National until May 1969. In 1973 it was exported to Wisconsin, USA.

This Royal Blue service was being operated by a 1955 Commer sporting a Harrington C41C body.

840 SUO, Fleet Number 2354, was a Bristol RE with ECW coachwork. It was delivered to Western National in 1964 where it served until 1977, when it was sold to Hants & Dorset, who broke it up for spares.

Shearings

Shearings, a common sight on today's roads, has a long and complicated history. The present day's company is an amalgamation of Smiths Happiways, National Holidays and Wallace Arnold. All of these also had complicated histories with takeovers and amalgamations of their own.

Smiths Happiways can trace its history back over 100 years. In 1914 James Smith started operating tours from Wigan and Southport. In 1931 he was bought out by William Webster, who had been running haulage and passenger-carrying businesses, also in Wigan, since 1903. A new company, James Smith and Co. (Wigan) Ltd was formed. Their tours were marketed by Websters Tours. They claim to be the first company to operate continental tours after the end of the Second World War, with a fourteen-day tour to Switzerland in 1946.

1958 saw another change of ownership when it was purchased by Les Gleave, and renamed Smiths Tours. This in turn was sold to Wilf Blundell of Southport in 1964. Wilf had started his business operating just one coach in 1950, and expanded by purchasing Enterprise Coaches in 1955, Poole's Coaches in 1958 and Tootle's Tours in 1960. He then purchased Spencer's Tours and Happiway Tours

A 1989 Leyland Tiger with Duple bodywork bore Shearing's fleet number 508.

from Edwin Holden in 1968. He merged these to create Happiway-Spencers Ltd. In 1980, this became Smiths Happiway-Spencers Ltd.

Herbert Shearing started his own coaching business in Oldham in 1919. In 1935 he expanded by taking over Eniway Motor Tours in 1935. They ran express coaches between Manchester and London. He retired in 1949 when his business was split into two companies, Shearings Tours (Manchester) Ltd and Shearings Tours (Oldham) Ltd. In 1953 they were both sold to James Robinson, who already owned Happiway Tours Ltd. In 1964 it was then sold to the Jackson family of Altringham, who already owned Pleasureways. The coaches were branded Shearings-Pleasureways-Ribblesdale, shortened to Shearings Ribblesdale in 1979 and finally Shearings Holidays in 1982.

In 1982 Associated Leisure acquired Smiths Happiway-Spencers and, two years later, they bought Shearings Holidays. Later that year Associated Leisure was purchased by Pleasurama. 1985 saw Pleasurama's Coaches being rebranded Smiths Shearings.

National Holidays had been established in 1976 as part of the National Bus Company. Ten years later, when the company was privatised again, National Holidays was sold to Pleasurama. Their coaches were rebranded Shearings National in 1989. The same year, Pleasurama became part of the Mecca Leisure Group in 1989. This in turn was taken over by the Rank Organisation the following year. The company continued to expand by taking over other coach companies.

In 2005 venture capitalists 3i, who already by that time owned Wallace Arnold, bought a controlling stake in Shearings, merging the two under the brand WA Shearings. In 2007 the 'WA' was dropped from the name on the coaches, although travel agents continued with the Wallace Arnold name.

Southdown

Southdown Motor Services was formed in 1915 by the amalgamation of Worthing Motor Services, the London & South Coast Haulage Company and the country services of the Brighton, Hove & Preston United Omnibus Company.

After the First World War, Southdown concentrated on expanding its bus business and coaching took a back seat, but in 1929/30 they purchased sixty-nine chassis purely for coaching purposes. The Eastbourne firm of Chapmans was also taken over about the same time. Chapman's was a long-established local company that started life running horse-drawn buses. With the advent of motorised charabancs they started running tours and in 1914 were the first company in the country to operate a tour that included hotel accommodation. The success of this first tour to Cornwall was soon followed by trips to Wales and other destinations.

A 1938 Harrington-bodied Leyland Cub, capable of seating the twenty-six passengers on a tour organised by Southdown Enthusiasts Club.

Day tours were also popular, with promenades of resorts including Eastbourne and Worthing having ranks where coaching companies could park and advertise their trips. Southdown shared these ranks with other coach companies, but their reputation for service and reliability gave them the edge over their competitors.

Express services were another source of revenue, with the first services linking south coast towns with the capital, but in 1932 a new service was introduced linking all the south coast resorts between Margate and Bournemouth. This service was called the South Coast Express and shared with East Kent and Royal Blue.

1950 saw the company's first overseas tour with a seventeen-day tour to France and Switzerland operated by Leyland Tiger 1223. The following year the vehicle was sent to Ireland, where it was used to operate a number of tours there.

In their early days, Southdown favoured chassis produced by Tilling Stevens, with bodies made by Shorts, Harringtons or Tillings but, in 1930, Leyland Tiger chassis were bought. These were bodied by London Lorries or Harringtons, a local company based in Hove. The latter's bodies were more stylish, and the interiors were superior, coming complete with curtains, comfortable seats and plush fittings.

1265 (HUF 5) was one of a batch of only six Leyland Tiger PS1 chassis to be bodied by Harrington. It was pictured on Brighton seafront behind a sister vehicle.

1809 (LCD 209) was a 1951 Leyland Royal Tiger, fitted with a Duple body. It was only capable of carrying twenty-six passengers, with rows of two seats on one side and one on the other. It was used on tours until 1962, after which it was only used for ordinary coach work. It was sold in 1966.

A radical new design was introduced in 1952/53. These were Leyland Royal Tigers. Their engines were mounted underneath the floor, which gave more room for passengers. They were designed for express work and incorporated a sliding roof. Fifty were introduced.

The company stayed loyal to Leyland with Leopards replacing the Tigers in the 1960s. Coupled with the local firm of Harrington's new, stylish Cavalier body, a new modern look was portrayed. The company continued to equip the vehicles to the highest standards to ensure that Southdown kept its reputation of supplying a comfortable reliable service.

In 1965 Southdown took delivery of ten more Leyland Leopards. These were supplied with the last bodies that Harrington's ever made, as the firm ceased production thereafter.

The early 1970s saw the last coaches to be delivered to the company. These were Leyland Leopards. Twenty, 1800–1819, had Duple Commander IV bodies and the final twenty-five had Plaxton Panorama Elite bodies, 1820–1844. These were the last coaches to be delivered in Southdown's two-tone green livery. There were more Leyland Leopards delivered, but these were in the NBC's green-and-white livery.

The company became part of the National Bus Company in 1969 and its name disappeared completely in 1989 when it was acquired by Stagecoach.

Known as a 'Beadle Rebuild', these were pre-war Leyland Tiger chassis, lengthened to 30 feet and fitted with a new body. There were twenty vehicles (850–869) converted to this mid-bodied entrance door, with a further thirty (870–899) having front entrances on a 26-foot chassis.

This example of a 1952 Leyland Royal Tiger 1634 (LUF 634) sported a Leyland body. 1600–1619 had Duple Ambassador bodies, while 1645–1649 had Duple Coronation Ambassador bodies. The destination blind was fitted in 1961 – four years before it was withdrawn.

Another Tiger Cub, this time a 1962 version, fitted with a Weymann Fanfare body.

A 1959-built Commer TS3 Avenger IV chassis with a body supplied by Burlingham, pictured at Chichester depot. It served until 1971 when it was sold.

After the Tigers came the Leopards. This is a 1962 Leyland Leopard with a Harringtons Cavalier body.

A 1966 Leyland Leopard with a Plaxton Panorama body, fitted with forty-nine passenger seats.

Another Plaxton-bodied Leyland leopard delivered in 1968, but lacking the brightwork of the vehicle in the top photo, and painted in a single shade of Southdown apple-green paint.

Wallace Arnold

Mr Wallace and Mr Arnold ran a charabanc business in Yorkshire in the early 1920s. However, it was not these two gentlemen who grew their business into one of the largest coach companies in the country. This is because, in 1926, they sold their business to Mr Robert Barr for £800.

Mr Barr already owned his own haulage business and he decided to keep his new coaching company as a separate entity and run it using the name of its founders. His original aim was to open up the countryside to all the townsfolk. He had been brought up on a farm and, after moving to the city of Leeds to find work, was appalled at the urban conditions compared to the countryside. However, most of his tours were outside the financial reach of the normal working class man and it was the middle classes that made up the majority of his clientele. When he took over his new company, they were already running tours to London and Edinburgh, using solid-tyre charabancs.

By 1928 he had modernised the fleet, which by then consisted entirely of all-weather coaches running on pneumatic tyres. The speed limit had been raised from 12 mph to 20 mph, and this opened up more routes that could be made in greater comfort. In 1933 their list of destinations was expanded to include continental destinations.

The company expanded rapidly, mainly by purchasing rival firms in the Yorkshire area. The Second World War brought an end to this expansion. Some coaches were requisitioned for the war effort, but other coaches were used for war work, so the business continued. They even purchased Wilks & Meade, a firm of coachbuilders, which proved a very astute move.

The post-war years brought a boom in leisure travel, and the company found it hard to keep up with demand. More new vehicles were purchased, more companies were bought out and their acquisition of a coachbuilders meant that they could repair and update older existing vehicles in their fleet. The fleet consisted of a number of different manufacturers, with a variety of bodies.

Until the late 1940s, the company had based its operations in the north but, in 1948, it acquired Homeland Tours of Croydon, which gave it a base in the more affluent south.

The company continued to run express coach services throughout the 1950s and these accounted for a substantial part of its business, with over 80,000 passengers being carried in 1959. With the advent of under-floor-engine vehicles in the 1950s, the extra space allowed more seats to be fitted and full fronts to be fitted, which meant that the older half-cabs began to look very dated. Wallace Arnold re-bodied many of its older coaches, while standardising on the new engine arrangement with new purchases.

WA were renowned for running successful, well-organised tours to top hotels in many seaside resorts, but it was a very short season. To extend the season,

A 1958 AEC Reliance with Plaxton Consort II bodywork. This vehicle has been preserved.

tours aimed at pensioners were planned at the start and end of the season. These were cut-price tours, but the standard of accommodation was much lower. Many other operators followed their lead in running off-season tours.

Robert Barr died in 1961 and his son, Malcolm, succeeded him as chairman.

The 1960s saw the company operating over 320 coaches from fifty-two locations. 869 employees helped make a gross profit of nearly half a million pounds.

The 1970s bought harder times for WA. They were faced with increasing competition from other large rivals, including Smiths Happiway-Spencers and Shearings-Pleasureway-Ribblesdale. National Holidays, which was part of the National Bus Company, was improving its services and gaining more market share.

Prior to 1980, all coaching was regulated and coaching companies had to apply for licences to run any trip they operated. This included listing any pick-up points and detailing the routes to be followed. These applications were often challenged by rival operators. Hearings were held to apply for licences and these took up a huge amount of time and involved masses of paperwork. The 1980 Transport Act put an end to all this red tape and operators were largely free to run where and when they liked. These changes, which helped WA with its paperwork, also helped smaller operators get started and expand their operations.

Wallace Arnold owned this 2001 Volvo B10M, fitted with a Plaxton body.

A 1987 Wallace Arnold Volvo B10M with Plaxton Paramount coachwork.

The 1980s saw the cutting back in some areas, and garages in Castleford, Royston, Bradford and Pudsey were all closed with the operation being centralised in Leeds. In 1984 a bid to take over the company from Smiths-Shearings was rejected. From 1985, the company bought its own hotels gaining more control over its operations. Also in 1985, the new Transport Act meant that all National Bus Companies had to be sold off to the private sector. Smiths-Shearings, which was part of the Pleasureways Group, acquired National Holidays. This company was virtually unknown in the south of England and this led to an increase in WA's business.

However, in the mid-1990s, the Barr family was divided in the way the company should proceed and it was decided to split the coaching from the haulage business (they had both been under the control of the Barr & Wallace Arnold Trust for some years) and they were both sold as individual businesses.

Despite rumours that Shearings would be the successful buyer, it was actually sold in 1997 to venture capitalists 3i. These venture capitalists also purchased Shearings. Both companies continued to exist, with much investment being poured into both companies, but, in 2005, the companies were merged and the famous Wallace Arnold coaches disappeared from our roads.

Smaller Companies

Although there were some large coaching companies, there were many smaller, perhaps family-run, businesses. It was, and still is, a field where a good living can be made with a few vehicles. This is probably partly due to the fact that there are not too many economies of scale that can be achieved and that most

Coliseum Coaches of Surrey owned this AEC Reliance with Duple Britannia coachwork.

small or medium-sized towns will only support a small company. These smaller firms often bought vehicles to their own specification that differed from the fleets purchased by the larger companies. This made their coaches more interesting and quirky, so I've included a few examples here.

Hawkeys of Cornwall owned this AEC Regal sporting Harrington's coachwork.

Universal Cars of Hertford owned this rare rear-engine Foden with a Windover body.

This Commer with Beadle bodywork was owned by Yorkshire Woollen.

Yeates built this Riviera style body, fitted to a Bedford chassis. The motif on the front says DWJ but I have not been able to ascertain what it stood for.

Taking the Kingswear Ferry was this Grey Car's Commer Beadle. It was delivered in 1956. Its distinctive engine note was made by a Commer TS3 two-stroke engine.

Dating from the early 1950s, Lewis owned this unusual vehicle. It was built by Sentinel, who constructed their own chassis and bodywork.

The Foreign Invasion

With the closure of many famous British coachbuilders and chassis makers, the door was left open for manufacturers on the continent to fulfil the orders of large and small coach operators. Volvo of Sweden, DAF and Bova of Holland and Mercedes and Setra of Germany were only too pleased to fill the gaps left by the demise of British manufacturers.

RJT 671 has been used on more than one coach. It is seen here on a DAF with Bova coachwork. In another life, it could be seen on a Plaxton-bodied Volvo, owned by Patron Travel of Nottinghamshire.

This was one of two Auwaerter Neoplan Skyliners in Harrods livery and owned by Eurocare of Richmond. They were employed on round London sightseeing tours.

Hams Travel of East Sussex owned this Volvo with Irizar body, pictured outside Tunbridge Wells Station in 2001. (Photo Courtesy Michael Clarke)

Globus Gateway operated this Van Hool-bodied DAF. (Photo Courtesy Michael Clarke)

Globus had modernised their livery when this photo was taken of their 2004-registered Setra.